December

She Walked
With Jesus

She Walked With Jesus

Stories of Christ Followers in the Bible

By Brenda Poinsett

new
hope
PUBLISHERS

Birmingham, Alabama

New Hope® Publishers
P. O. Box 12065
Birmingham, AL 35202-2065
www.newhopepubl.com

Library of Congress Cataloging-in-Publication Data
Poinsett, Brenda.
She walked with Jesus : stories of Christ followers in the Bible / by Brenda Poinsett.
p. cm.
Includes bibliographical references.
ISBN 1-56309-830-X (softcover)
1. Bible. N.T.-Biography. 2. Women in the Bible-Biography. 3.
Christian women-Religious life. I. Title.
BS575.P65 2004
225.9'2'082—dc22
2003025676

Unless otherwise noted, Scriptures are taken from the Good News Bible in Today's English Version—Second Edition, Copyright © 1992 by American Bible Society. Used by permission.

Scripture quotations marked (CEV) are taken from the Contemporary English Version. Copyright © 1995 American Bible Society.

Scripture quotations marked (KJV) are taken from The Holy Bible, King James Version.

Scripture quotations marked (NKJV) are taken from the New King James Version. Copyright © 1982 by Thomas Nelson, Inc. Used by permission. All rights reserved.

Scripture quotations marked (NASB) are taken from the NEW AMERICAN STANDARD BIBLE®, Copyright © 1960, 1962, 1963, 1968, 1971, 1972, 1973, 1975, 1977, 1995 by The Lockman Foundation. Used by permission.

Scripture quotations marked (NIV) are taken from the HOLY BIBLE, NEW INTERNATIONAL VERSION®. NIV®. Copyright©1973, 1978, 1984 by International Bible Society. Used by permission of Zondervan. All rights reserved.

Scripture quotations marked (RSV) are taken from the Revised Standard Version of the Bible, copyright 1952 [2nd edition, 1971] by the Division of Christian Education of the National Council of the Churches of Christ in the U.S.A. Used by permission. All rights reserved.

Scripture quotations marked (NRSV) are taken from the New Revised Standard Version Bible, copyright 1989, by the Division of Christian Education of the National Council of the Churches of Christ in the U.S.A. Used by permission. All rights reserved.

Scripture quotations marked (ESV) are from The Holy Bible, English Standard Version, copyright © 2001 by Crossway Bibles, a division of Good News Publishers. Used by permission. All rights reserved.

ISBN: 1-56309-830-X

N044103 • 0504 • 10M1

Dedication

To
Jan Turner
Linda Magruder
and
Janet Hofer

table of contents

Acknowledgments

Many kind people helped with the development of this book, and I want to acknowledge them and express my appreciation.

First, I want to thank the students who took my class "Women of the Bible" at Oakland City University's Bedford, Indiana, campus. It was a rigorous study—one I probably wouldn't have done on my own, but our journey together opened my eyes to many Bible women I had not noticed before. I wouldn't have wanted to miss knowing them.

Thanks, too, to the Department Club of Bedford who asked me to speak to them about women of the Bible. I selected some New Testament women to share with them, and the club members responded with, "That ought to be in a book." So the seed was planted and I knew that someday I wanted to write a book about these women.

Still, that wouldn't have been possible without some recommendations along the line. I'm grateful to Sheryl Churchill, Laura Savage, Kathy Scott, Becky Yates, and Rebecca England for passing on my name at the right time in various places so that I might be the author of this book.

When it came to help with the actual writing, I'm grateful to Pat McAlister, who read and critiqued some of the early chapter drafts, to Barbara Williams, who helped me sort out my thinking about older women in the church, to my husband Bob for listening to stories of Christ followers over dinner, to my son Ben for his encouragement, and to Rebecca England for a great job of editing and answering questions along the way. Thanks also to Kenneth Steffen, Ministry by Mail Coordinator of Roberts Library, who provided me with helpful resources to better understand the stories of women who followed Christ. It's a better book because of their help.

Thanks to many friends for their prayers: Debbie Hawkins, Susan Miller, Jan Turner, Linda Magruder, Debbie Miller, Vivian McCaughn, Annette Huber, Barbara Popp, and Mary Rose Fox. Others, such as members of my church, the First Baptist Church of St. Clair, Missouri's WMU Board, and my October women retreat committee, were praying for me when I didn't even know. I am touched and grateful they would pray.

Like the "Women of the Bible" course mentioned above, the class I wouldn't have wanted to miss, I wouldn't have wanted to miss the experience of writing this book about Christ followers. I've learned from them and at the same time have had my life and work enriched by many good, thoughtful people. I am blessed.

Introduction:
Women Who Followed Christ

John Grisham's novel *The Testament* begins with an eccentric billionaire committing suicide. All of his heirs are anxious to receive what they believe to be their rightful inheritance. His lawyers, though, discover in his will that the bulk of his wealth is to go to Rachel Lane, an illegitimate daughter whom the other heirs knew nothing about. The billionaire had had little contact with Rachel. He didn't even know exactly where she was, only that she was a missionary somewhere in South America. Finding her became the task of one of the lawyers, Nate, who had a checkered past and was fresh out of alcohol rehab. When Nate found Rachel, he met a woman at peace with herself, unselfishly ministering to Indians, and—shockingly to the lawyer and others—uninterested in inheriting billions of dollars.

A review in a major Christian magazine gave *The Testament* high marks, except for Rachel. The reviewer said Rachel was too good to be true. She was "unworldly, unselfish, and totally unbelievable."

I raised my eyebrow at the comment because I had already read *The Testament* and I had found Rachel believable. I was pleased to see in the next issue a letter to the editor from someone who agreed with me.

> "I would like to take issue with the reviewer's contention that Grisham's character, the missionary Rachel, is 'unworldly, unselfish, and totally unbelievable.' My sister was a missionary, and while I knew Grisham had never met her, I found that fact hard to believe. His Rachel is so like my sister it is uncanny. Believe me, there are many unworldly and unselfish missionaries, unremarked and unknown, serving God around the world."

I would go so far as to say there are not only many missionaries like Rachel, there are many unselfish and unworldly women following Christ, quietly serving, being faithful, going unrecognized by the larger Christian community. I know because I see them everywhere I go.

Women Who Are Out of This World

I'm a speaker and a women's ministries consultant, so I interact with women on many different occasions and in a variety of places. I've also moved a lot, and in the process I've been a member of various kinds of churches—large, small, and in between. Among the Christian women I've met, I've identified a group who resemble each other and who resemble Christ.

The women don't physically look like each other, but there is something about them that makes me connect them to each other and to Christ.

I distinctly remember the first time I made this connection. I was outside, visiting with a neighbor in a new community. As we chatted about our children and the neighborhood, I sensed that I knew this woman or that I had at least met her before. I quizzed her about the places she lived. As we compared backgrounds, it became clear that our paths had never crossed.

Then it occurred to me that perhaps she was a Christian. She wasn't carrying a Bible, nor had she used any religious language, but her mannerisms and her demeanor made me think "Christian," so I asked her, "Are you a Christian?"

Her face broke into a big smile, and she answered, "Why, yes I am."

Well, that answer certainly gave us more to talk about! And it also gave me more to think about as I went back into the house. Why had I had the sense of knowing her? Had she merely reminded me of some one person? If so, who? She didn't look like anyone I knew. As I pondered this, faces of women from past places I had lived came to mind. They didn't all look like my neighbor, and even though I didn't know my new neighbor very well, these women didn't all act like her or each other. As I looked for a word that would connect them, which would describe them all, I batted around *humble, good, faithful, loyal, serving, earnest, obedient, unselfish, cooperative,* and *dedicated.* They had the attitude that the apostle Paul encouraged us to have, the attitude of Jesus. Paul wrote, "Of his own free will he gave up all he had, and took the nature of a servant" (Philippians 2:7), and that "He was humble and walked the path of obedience" (Philippians 2:8).

Of their own free will, these women became servants—serving Jesus Christ and others in His name. They were humble, and they faithfully walked the path of obedience. They followed Christ in many different ways, but it was plain that they knew Him, that they had been transformed by Him. The fact that they were Christ followers showed in their person, in their actions, and in their demeanor.

I see some of these women in leadership roles, but more often I find them in supportive roles. They staff the church nursery, handle Vacation Bible School, prepare funeral dinners, teach Sunday school, wipe the tears of the hurting, lead the church's missions emphasis, organize prayer chains, and plan luncheons where speakers speak. They are not usually "stars," the celebrities of the Christian world, receiving much attention, praise, and applause. No one lines up to get their autographs or have their pictures taken with them. Some will live and die without their work ever being noticed.

I think we should notice these Christ followers, and here are two reasons why. First, I need these women in my life. I need real examples of what it means today if we take seriously Jesus' words: "If any of you want to be my followers, you must forget about yourself. You must take up your cross each day and follow me" (Luke 9:23 CEV). And second, I want to become like these women. My culture won't help me become more like Jesus—they probably won't even believe it when they see it. It's too different from what the world teaches us to strive for. We need other Christians to help us understand what it means to follow Christ today.

How about you? Do you need the example of other women who followed Christ? If so, then come along with me, as we take a look at some women who were Christ followers.

The 1st Century-21st Century Link

The women we are going to look at lived in the first century, during or very soon after that time when Jesus, the Son of God, came into the world, lived, worked, preached, taught, and healed. He died on a cross and was raised to life again on the third day. The good news about the power of the cross and the resurrection spread and people believed. Those who believed banded together and called themselves the church. They were Christ followers, living and working together to follow His direction to be witnesses in Jerusalem, Judea, and Samaria, and the uttermost parts of the world.

We will look at three women whose expectant faith

cradled the birth of Jesus—Elizabeth, Mary of Nazareth, and Anna. They "nested" His appearance, and in who they were, we see the heart of a Christ follower.

We will look at the ministries of women who followed Christ—the Galilean women, Mary Magdalene, Mary and Martha of Bethany, and the women at the cross. These women actually knew Jesus. They knew Him firsthand, and as we look at their stories, we will feel as if we are having firsthand experiences as we see Jesus through their eyes.

Then we will look at the relationships of women who were among the first Christians—Dorcas, Lydia, Lois and Eunice, Priscilla, Phoebe, Titus' helpers, and Timothy's widows. We will see how women followed Jesus in the early days of the church. Jesus was no longer with them in the flesh, but He was with them in Spirit, much the same as He is for us today. Looking at the stories of these Christ followers will help us feel His presence and help us learn to follow Him as they did.

When we step into the shoes of these women, we are getting in step with Jesus to be true Christ followers. I encourage you to find the women you relate to, whose personality or giftedness or circumstances are similar to yours. These stories are to encourage and inspire you, not Jell-O-mold you into something. Find some women to be your role models and inspiration.

Of course, what happened to me may happen to you—I identified with them all! We connected across the centuries that divide us. They added to my understanding of what it means to follow Christ, they inspired me, and yes, they became my friends. I hope they become your friends, too, and that together we become more devoted Christ followers.

chapter one

Elizabeth:
A Christ Follower
Waits and Hopes

*Luke 1:5–45,
56–66*

Elizabeth has the distinction of being the only woman called righteous in the New Testament. Not only was Elizabeth called good, but so also was her husband. The Bible says that Elizabeth and Zechariah "lived good lives in God's sight and obeyed fully all the Lord's laws and commands" (Luke 1:6). The King James Version says they "were both righteous before God."

What exactly does that mean? In her book *Women in the New Testament*, Mary Ann Getty-Sullivan explains, "To be righteous meant to be focused on God and on the will of God as revealed in the

Law." Elizabeth, whose name means "God is my treasure," or "God is the one by whom I swear," did this unquestioningly even though there must have been times when she wanted to ask questions.

God, Why Am I Childless?

Many girls grow up dreaming of the day when they will be mothers; this was especially true of Jewish girls, because bearing children was very important. Children brought joy to a home. Children provided security for the later years. Children were a sign of God's favor. Children carried on your name, passed on your faith and rituals, and inherited your property. A woman's worth and hope were measured by her children. Elizabeth had no children.

I imagine that Elizabeth couldn't help but think about her childlessness whenever she said goodbye to Zechariah. He was a priest, and periodically he had to leave their home in the hill country of Judea and go to the Temple in Jerusalem to help with the daily services. Elizabeth didn't begrudge his leaving; she was the daughter of a priest and she understood the importance of his role.

As she watched him pack his bags, she thanked God for Zechariah. Other women who couldn't conceive were not as fortunate—their husbands divorced them. In those days, a Jewish man could do that if his wife had no child. Childlessness was considered valid grounds for divorce. If a couple did not conceive, then the blame—and shame—always fell on the woman, but Zechariah had stayed with Elizabeth. Together they focused on God and His will and prayed that they would have a child.

Elizabeth must have felt wistful as she watched Zechariah walk down the hill. As she walked back into the house, it seemed so quiet. What would her life be like if Zechariah didn't come home? What if something happened to him? She would have no one to help her, no son to support her as a widow. For years they had hoped for a child, but how long do you keep hoping? She was tempted to ask, "God, why? Why couldn't I have a child? Why couldn't I experience the joy of motherhood?" Then she shook her head to shake the questions out of her mind. She smiled to herself, *Must be old age that is making me think like this. I really feel the weight of the years this morning.*

Elizabeth's circumstances were such that she could have become disillusioned, but she didn't. She lived up to her name. God is the one she swore by. That's why when Zechariah left for Jerusalem, her last words to him probably were, "Now don't worry about me. I will be okay."

Joy in Jerusalem

When Zechariah arrived at the Temple, he learned he had been chosen to burn incense on the altar (Luke 1:9). He went into the Temple while people gathered outside as they usually did to pray during the hour the incense burned.

As he was going about his duties, an angel appeared,

standing at the right side of the altar where the incense was burning. What a startling surprise! In all his years of serving in the Temple, nothing like this had ever happened. Zechariah "was alarmed and felt afraid" (Luke 1:12).

The angel, Gabriel, quickly reassured him, "Don't be afraid, Zechariah! God has heard your prayer, and your wife Elizabeth will bear you a son. You are to name him John" (Luke 1:13).

Zechariah must have experienced sensory overload. The incense aroma, the angel's sudden appearance, the fear that clutched him, the angel's reassurance, confirmation that his prayer was heard, and the announcement that he and Elizabeth were going to have a child were almost too much for him. His heart beat fast and he felt as if he might faint. He rubbed his forehead, trying to absorb what was being said, and then Gabriel said more!

"How glad and happy you will be, and how happy many others will be when he is born! He will be a great man in the Lord's sight. He must not drink any wine or strong drink. From his very birth he will be filled with the Holy Spirit, and he will bring back many of the people of Israel to the Lord their God. He will go ahead of the Lord, strong and mighty like the prophet Elijah. He will bring fathers and children together again; he will turn disobedient people back to the way of thinking of the righteous; he will get the Lord's people ready for him" (Luke 1:14–17).

About this time, Zechariah raised a doubtful question. The angel's words didn't jive with reality.

"Zechariah said to the angel, 'How shall I know if this is so? I am an old man, and my wife is old also'" (Luke 1:18).

Gabriel replied, "I stand in the presence of God, who sent me to speak to you and tell you this good news. But you have not believed my message, which will come true at the right time. Because you have not believed, you will be unable to speak; you will remain silent until the day my promise to you comes true" (Luke 1:19–20).

Now Zechariah was frustrated as well as perplexed. He couldn't talk! And the people were waiting outside of the Temple's court of the priests. They were waiting in the court of the Israelites for his blessing. Reeling from what he'd learned, he was confused and bewildered, yet also happy and exhilarated. How could he bless the people? How could he tell them what happened when he couldn't say a word?

The people were already anxious because Zechariah had stayed in the court of priests longer than usual. When he finally came out and no sounds came from Zechariah's mouth, they knew something unusual had happened. They assumed he had seen a vision. Unable to say a word, he made signs to them with his hands. The hand signals may have conveyed a blessing but certainly didn't explain completely what happened. As he started home, he must have wondered, *How will I tell Elizabeth?* Even if he could verbalize, he didn't know if he could find the words to explain the extraordinary experience he had.

Back Home to Elizabeth

When Elizabeth saw Zechariah coming up the hill, she knew something had happened. His countenance was changed and his forehead was wrinkled. He looked pale. Elizabeth ran to meet him. "What? What?" she asked. And then Zechariah really felt the limitations of his handicap. He wanted so much to tell her what happened. He made motions, like the gestures he made in Jerusalem, but they were inadequate. He got out a tablet and he began to write—a little here and a little there—until he told Elizabeth every detail.

She raised an eyebrow a time or two in surprise as she read his words. Elizabeth believed Zechariah and she believed God. Her heart beat with the certainty that God was at last fulfilling her heart's desire. Sure enough, some time later, she became pregnant. "'Now at last the Lord has helped me,' she said. 'He has taken away my public disgrace!'" (Luke 1:25).

Oddly—and I say oddly because you would think Elizabeth would want to tell everyone her good news—she responded to her pregnancy by going into seclusion. She hid herself for five months. Why she did this is a puzzle to Bible commentators because they know of no Palestinian custom that would call for seclusion. Some attribute theological significance to her seclusion. She had to stay hidden until the plan of salvation reached the point at which it was to be made known; that is, when Mary became pregnant with Jesus.

I can think of some other logical reasons.

Elizabeth had waited a long time to become pregnant, and the Bible more than once describes her as "very old." She may have been uneasy by the physical changes that occurred when she became pregnant. At her age, the morning sickness, the sleepiness, and the mood shifts in the early months might have been disconcerting, and she felt more comfortable staying to herself.

Perhaps she felt her age was a point of too much interest on the part of others. Maybe she feared if she went out in public she would be talked about. "There goes Elizabeth. I've heard she is pregnant. Can you imagine having a child *at her age?*"

On the other hand, maybe the experience was so precious to her that she wanted to keep it to herself. After so many years of waiting, God was doing a wonderful thing in her life. She wanted to hug the experience close and not have other people discuss it or dissect it. She wanted to be alone so she could relish her pregnancy and spend time in reverent wonder at what God was doing in her and Zechariah's life. She wanted to marvel at the kind of child their union was going to produce. There was a lot to think about. The miraculous was occurring as the baby grew in Elizabeth's womb. But another miracle was also about to happen.

Gabriel Speaks Again

Six months after the angel Gabriel appeared to Zechariah, he appeared to Mary in Nazareth of Galilee. This angelic visit was not in the sanctuary of the great Temple, but in the quiet of a humble home. It was not to a priest wearing rich garments, but to a young woman of modest means. It was not to a married person, but to a young virgin engaged to be married to Joseph, a carpenter and a descendant of King David.

Gabriel said to Mary, "Rejoice, highly favored one, the Lord is with you; blessed are you among women!" (Luke 1:28 NKJV).

Mary pondered the greeting. What did it mean?

Gabriel assured her that she had found favor with God. God was blessing her. Gabriel then made a startling announcement: "You will become pregnant and give birth to a son, and you will name him Jesus. He will be great and will be called the Son of the Most High God" (Luke 1:31–32).

Mary did not doubt, but she was puzzled. She said, "I am a virgin. How, then, can this be?"

Gabriel explained that the conception would be an act of the Holy Spirit. The creative power of God would overshadow her and make this possible.

Still, the idea of becoming pregnant without knowing a man seemed impossible to Mary. Gabriel reassured her by telling her about another supernatural happening. He said, "Remember your relative Elizabeth. It is said that she cannot have children, but she herself is now six months pregnant, even though she is very old. For there is nothing that God cannot do" (Luke 1:36–37).

Hmm, thought Mary, *someone else is having a supernatural birth. I've got to talk to her.* So Mary hastened off to the hill country in Judea where Elizabeth lived. "Hello, hello, Elizabeth. Have I got something to tell you!"

The Spirit Moves

Mary knew about Elizabeth's condition because Gabriel told her, but Elizabeth didn't know about Mary's situation. Elizabeth did not know that Mary had a visit from the same angel that spoke to her husband. She didn't know that Mary was pregnant, even when she opened the door. The trip from Nazareth to Elizabeth's house in Judea took only a few days, so Mary's pregnancy wasn't visible yet. I mention this so you can see the full significance of what happens when Mary arrives.

When Elizabeth heard Mary's greeting, the baby moved within her. Movement at six months is certainly not anything unusual, but the timing and the force of the movement were. The movement coincided with Mary's greeting, as if the baby recognized Mary's voice. It was not a flutter; the baby "leaped in her womb" (Luke 1:41 NASB). The movement reminded Elizabeth of Gabriel's words to her husband about their baby: "he will be filled with the Holy Spirit while yet in his mother's womb" (Luke 1:15 NASB). The joy of this realization prompted a swelling of the Holy Spirit within Elizabeth, and she could put together what no one had spelled out for her.

From Zechariah's feeble communication, she had learned that their child would be like an Elijah, someone to prepare people for the day of the Lord. It would naturally follow that this meant the Anointed One would be coming soon. In that culture, people attributed conscious action even to unborn babies. When the sound of Mary's voice struck Elizabeth's ears her unborn child "leaped for joy" (NIV). Elizabeth realized Mary was the mother of the one for whom her son was to prepare the way.

Elizabeth was ecstatic. In a loud voice, she said to Mary, "You are the most blessed of all women, and blessed is the child you will bear! Why should this great thing happen to me, that my Lord's mother comes to visit me? For as soon as I heard your greeting, the baby within me jumped with gladness. How happy you are to believe that the Lord's message to you will come true!" (Luke 1:42–45).

Zechariah had his supernatural moment when Gabriel visited him in the Temple.

Mary had hers when Gabriel visited her in Nazareth.

And now Elizabeth had hers, and she was humbled by it. *Why should this great thing happen to me?* She was awed by the experience. It would be years before Elizabeth's child would announce Mary's child to the world, and Elizabeth might not live to see it, but she knew it would happen. She would stake her life on it. There was a certainty in her heart that all this was being orchestrated by God, a certainty that would prompt her to insist that her baby be called John, as the angel had said.

The Birthday Party

In Palestine, the birth of a child was an occasion of great joy. When Elizabeth gave birth, her neighbors and relatives gathered around to share in the excitement. They wanted to rejoice with her and Zechariah and celebrate the birth of the baby.

As pious Jews, Elizabeth and Zechariah fulfilled the

Law and arranged for their baby son to be circumcised on the eighth day as prescribed. The day of circumcision was also the day a boy received his name.

Those circumcising the baby planned to name him Zechariah after his father. This was the customary thing to do, and would be the logical thing in this case since Zechariah at his age probably would not have any more sons.

After the circumcision was performed would have come the pronouncement of grace: "Our God and the God of our fathers, raise up this child to his father and mother, and let his name be called in Israel Zechariah, the son of Zechariah."

But Elizabeth interrupted the pronouncement. She said, "No, his name is to be John."

The group was startled by her objection. John was not even a family name among the kin of Zechariah and Elizabeth. Her suggestion was so inappropriate, that the group would not accept it. They complained. "But you don't have any relatives with that name!" Even though Elizabeth was the mother, her word was not enough; they asked Zechariah.

Zechariah requested his writing pad. On it, he wrote, "His name is John," a shorter form of the name Jehohanan, which means "Jehovah's gift" or "God is gracious." The angel, sent by God, had told them to name the child John—and the name also described Elizabeth and Zechariah's gratitude for their unexpected joy.

Barren No Longer

Elizabeth had lived with a situation that could have caused her to be disillusioned about God and bitter about life. Instead she chose to keep her focus on God and on doing His will, and she did this with a sense of expectancy and hope. What we have seen in Elizabeth, I have seen in many women who live with a painful or disappointing aspect of their life and yet still follow Christ.

An infertile woman works with the children of others and teaches them about a God who answers prayer.

A woman whose husband is not a believer serves God faithfully and cheerfully year after year and seldom misses a Sunday church service, even though she worships alone.

A mother of a prodigal daughter looks expectantly every day for her to return home while she teaches teenagers in Sunday school and prepares them for life.

A single woman who has dreamed for years of being a wife and mother is known on the job for her high performance and is admired for her Christian witness.

A Sunday school teacher claims the promises of God, but never sees those promises fulfilled. Her class doesn't grow. The Spirit doesn't move among the students. Lives don't change. She doesn't understand why, but she continues to teach God's promises to others.

These women offer examples of waiting on the Lord. They wait not with a sense of resignation but with a vitality of hopefulness and expectancy. It's a waiting that doesn't let faith wilt on the vine. It's a waiting that sees God as gracious and kind, even when life is unfair.

It's a waiting that says even if part of my life is not what I desire, I desire God and want to follow Him.

I cannot promise that God will respond to waiting women in the same way that He responded to Elizabeth, fulfilling her unfilled desire, but I can promise that God will meet them in the process. "He rewards those who earnestly seek him" (Hebrews 11:6 NIV). Some time, at some place, God will respond to you in such a way that you will wonder as Elizabeth did, "Why should this happen to me?"

chapter two

Mary of Nazareth:
A Christ Follower Submits to God's Will

Matthew 1 & 2
Matthew 12:46–50
Mark 3:31–35
Luke 1 & 2
Luke 8:19–21
John 2:1–11
John 19:25–27
Acts 1:14

Do you remember what Mary said when Gabriel told her that she would bear God's child? She said, "I am a virgin. How, then, can this be?"

"The angel answered, 'The Holy Spirit will come on you, and God's power will rest upon you" (Luke 1:35).

Without any regard for how this pregnancy might complicate her life, Mary said, "I am the Lord's servant…may it happen to me as you have said" (Luke 1:38). This was Mary's signature statement, reflecting her attitude about serving God. Although not actually stated again, we see over and over in her life that Mary's behavior matched this statement, through good times and bad.

The Good Times

Astonishing as Gabriel's news was, Mary submitted herself to the assignment with joy. She shared that joy with Elizabeth, who was also experiencing a miraculous pregnancy. What a precious time they must have had as they talked about babies and God's blessings! While visiting Elizabeth, Mary sang, "My heart praises the Lord; my soul is glad because of God my Savior, for he has remembered me, his lowly servant! From now on all people will call me happy, because of the great things the Mighty God has done for me" (Luke 1:46–49).

Their "girl talk" may have included some apprehension on Mary's part. She was engaged to Joseph. Would he still marry her when he found out she was pregnant? Would he believe that her pregnancy was by God's Spirit?

When she returned to Nazareth, she found out that God had already taken care of her concern. An angel of the Lord had appeared to Joseph in a dream. The angel said, "Do not be afraid to take Mary to be your wife. For it is by the Holy Spirit that she has conceived" (Matthew 1:20).

After their marriage they went to Bethlehem, just as Mary was about to deliver her child. Why travel during her pregnancy? Because the government had ordered a census for taxation purposes, and every man had to travel to his city of origin to be counted. While they were there,

Jesus was born. As Mary looked into His face, her heart filled with joy. *Oh, if only she and Joseph had someone to share their happiness with.*

Just as she was thinking this, shepherds arrived. They said they had been watching their flocks in the hills when an angel told them about Jesus' birth and a heavenly host sang praises. Their stories added to the wonder Mary felt at being God's handmaiden, chosen to bear His Son.

Later, some unusual visitors arrived. The visitors had traveled a long way, from the east, they said. They had even stopped by King Herod's in Jerusalem. Mary's maternal feelings swelled as she heard them say they wanted to see the baby born to be king of the Jews. When Mary showed Jesus to the visitors, they knelt down and worshiped Him. They gave Him gifts of gold, frankincense, and myrrh and told her that King Herod wanted to see the baby too. "He asked us to stop by on our return trip home to tell him where the Christ child was."

Not a somber note appeared on the horizon until Mary and Joseph took baby Jesus to the Temple in Jerusalem (Luke 2:22–38). A godly old man named Simeon received them. He took Jesus in his arms and said some wonderful things about Him—the kind of words that make a mother proud. Mary was beaming until Simeon said to her, "And sorrow, like a sharp sword, will break your own heart" (Luke 2:35). Caught off guard, Mary received the words just long enough to store them in her memory, and then forgot them as someone else exclaimed about the baby. She didn't know that in just a few days she would be reminded of Simeon's warning.

The Sword's First Sting

After Jesus' presentation at the Temple, Mary was ready to get back home to Nazareth. She was anxious to get settled. When she expressed her feelings to Joseph, he said, "I'm sorry, Mary, but we won't be going home. We're going to Egypt."

"Egypt! But that's so far away. I want to go home."

"We must go," said Joseph. "An angel of the Lord appeared to me in a dream and told me that Herod will be looking for Jesus in order to kill him. He doesn't really want to worship Jesus as the visitors from the East indicated. The angel insisted we go to Egypt. I don't understand it all either, my darling, but I know Herod is evil and I know for certain an angel of the Lord appeared to me."

"All right, Joseph. Whatever God says, I will do," Mary said, even though she had never lived outside Galilee except for those months when she visited Elizabeth. Now she was going to Egypt, where the culture was completely different and where they would be strangers in a foreign land. She winced, as she felt the tip of the sword of sorrow prick her skin.

Egypt wasn't so far away that Mary didn't hear about what happened back in Bethlehem. From travelers she learned that Herod had killed all boys two years old and younger. She was thankful Jesus was safe, but her heart ached for the mothers of the boys killed. Weeping, she wondered if she would have to live forever in Egypt. With a deep sigh, she prayed, "I am your servant, Lord. Wherever you want me to live, I will live."

When Herod died, an angel of the Lord appeared once

again in a dream to Joseph. The angel said, "Get up, take the child and his mother, and go back to the land of Israel, because those who tried to kill the child are dead" (Matthew 2:20).

So Joseph took Mary and Jesus back to Judea, thinking they would be safe now, but once there, Joseph heard that Archelaus had succeeded his father Herod as king. Archelaus was every bit as evil as his father, so, following more instructions from an angel in a dream, Joseph took his family on to Galilee, back to Nazareth. Mary was home at last.

What Kind of Child Is This?

Back home, back to the familiar, Mary and Joseph had more children, and life became ordinary and routine, just the way Mary liked it. Part of Mary and Joseph's routine was going to Jerusalem for the Passover each year. When Jesus was twelve, He was old enough to attend, so Mary and Joseph took Him with them.

The festival of Passover lasted seven days, but the main sacrifices were offered during the first two days; so on the third day most pilgrims began returning home. This is what the travelers from Nazareth did. A twelve-year-old was expected to take care of himself, so the company traveled a day before Mary and Joseph noticed Jesus' absence. They looked for Him among their relatives and friends, but they could not find Him, so they went back to Jerusalem to hunt for Him.

Mary and Joseph searched frantically through the city. Jesus was a bright young adolescent, the kind that brought slave traders high prices, and his parents were fearful. The worried parents finally found Jesus in the Temple, sitting with the Jewish teachers, asking—and answering—questions!

At first Mary and Joseph were incredulous. They couldn't believe what they were seeing and hearing. Around them people were making comments; they were amazed at Jesus' intelligent answers.

Jesus seemed oblivious to all the attention, as if it was the most natural thing in the world to be engaged in discussion with esteemed Jewish teachers.

His parents, on the other hand, could not understand why Jesus was unaware of their feelings and his responsibilities as a child. Mary said to him, "Son, why have you done this to us? Your father and I have been terribly worried trying to find you" (Luke 2:48).

Expecting some kind of credible explanation for His behavior, Mary was taken back by Jesus' answer. He said, "Why did you have to look for me? Didn't you know that I had to be in my Father's house?" (Luke 2:49).

Mary was shocked. This was a side of Jesus she hadn't seen before. From conception, Mary knew that Jesus was a special child, but in the routine of living, the sense of that had dulled, and now she was being forced to think. *What did Jesus mean about being in His Father's house? Why shouldn't they have looked for Him? How were they supposed to know where He was? Why were the people so amazed at His answers?* As Mary pondered these questions, she was confident that answers would ultimately come; she was the Lord's servant and she trusted Him.

Once a Mother, Always a Mother

One thing that became very clear to Mary that day in Jerusalem was the maturity of her first born. It was a maturity that she would marvel at—and rely on—through the years as she mothered a house full of children. Mary slipped easily into that groove that many mothers of cooperative, obedient children do. They depend on them and expect them to readily follow their commands, whether they are direct or inferred. Once in that groove, it is hard to step out of it. Even after Jesus was no longer living at home, Mary still counted on His help.

He had been away for several months in Judea and returned to Galilee with His disciples for a wedding that His mother was helping with. Mary was looking after the details of the event, wanting things to go well for the bride and groom on this important occasion. When she noticed the wine running out, Mary said to Jesus, "They are out of wine." Notice this is not a command as in "Jesus, please get some wine and save the bridal couple from being humiliated." The command is inferred: "Here's the situation, and I expect you do something and do it now."

Jesus got the message. It was clear! But He resisted complying. "'Dear woman, why do you involve me?' Jesus replied, 'My time has not yet come'" (John 2:4 NIV).

Unfazed by Jesus' response, Mary told the servants, "Do whatever he tells you" (John 2:5). She had confidence in her firstborn. She knew He would do something!

But what exactly did Mary expect Him to do? Go to a vineyard and buy more wine? Or had she seen Him do unusual things that hinted of the miraculous? Was His supernatural ability a secret they shared? Is that why He responded, "My time has not yet come?" Regardless, Jesus saw the time as premature for revealing His ability. Nevertheless, He had the servants fill the jars used for ritual washing with water, and He turned the water into very tasty wine.

In that act, Jesus' disciples and His brothers who were present saw a side of Him they had not seen before. Jesus had supernatural ability! What did this mean for His future? For theirs? Jesus, Mary, His brothers, and His disciples went to Capernaum to discuss the repercussions of this revelation. After a few days, Jesus and His disciples went back to Judea, and Mary and her sons returned to Nazareth. Mary was certain that Jesus' ability to perform miracles could only be a good thing; she was certain His future was bright.

A Mother's Concern

Wherever Jesus went, He attracted large crowds, and a primary reason for that attraction was that He performed miracles. His miracles changed people's lives and revealed Jesus' compassion, but they also caused Him to get a lot of attention. Some people followed Him just to see what would happen next.

The size of the crowds alarmed the Roman officials. They regarded anyone who could attract thousands as possible dissidents, and they had no qualms about punishing people they saw as threats to the empire.

Jewish officials, especially the religious leaders, also

became alarmed because people began talking about the possibility that Jesus might be the Messiah. When they checked Him out, they heard Jesus say things that challenged their sacred rules. This raised their ire and they determined to find a way to get rid of him. They joined the crowds surrounding Jesus, hoping to catch Him doing or saying something for which they could arrest Him.

When Jesus miraculously healed a man "possessed with a devil, blind and dumb," some religious leaders accused Jesus of being in league with Beelzebub, the prince of devils. Some people even said Jesus had gone mad (Mark 3:21).

When rumors of all of these things filtered back to Mary—especially the one about His going mad, she was ready to do something. Fearing both for Jesus' safety and His sanity, Mary was ready to go see Jesus and bring Him home. Forget ministry! Forget miracles! Forget mission! She was ready to issue another command. *Jesus, You need to come home!* She was taking action, and she took Her other sons along to help her.

I think it is important for us to see this side of Mary, see her as a woman taking action. Otherwise we might get the impression that Mary was a passive woman who agreed to anything; "whatever will be will be." Her submission to God's will was not robotic in nature, and if we believe that it was, we would underappreciate Mary. She had great privileges and responsibilities in God's redemptive plan, but her participation didn't always come easily. Her submission wasn't automatic. It involved consideration and struggle, and at times a personal cost, as you'll see.

A Mother's Perplexity

Jesus was inside a house, talking to people, when his mother and brothers arrived. They stood outside and sent a message in, asking to speak with Him. As all Jews would, Jesus' family members assumed that He would see them at their request. Who is going to refuse to see family? They waited expectantly.

But Jesus didn't break away and come to them. One of the people said to Jesus, "'Look, your mother and brothers are standing outside, and they want to speak with you.' Jesus answered, 'Who is my mother? Who are my brothers?' Then he pointed to his disciples and said, 'Look! Here are my mother and my brothers! Whoever does what my Father in heaven wants him to do is my brother, my sister, and my mother'" (Matthew 12:47–50).

When Mary and her sons heard Him, they were probably shocked and hurt. How could He insist that the closest human tie was not blood kinship, but the tie that exists between those who obey God? And how could He ignore them? The sword of sorrow twisted and turned inside her as it headed toward her heart.

Mary's journey home must have been a sad one. She had a lot to sort out. It was clear that Jesus had distanced Himself from His family. But she also knew Him well enough to know that He was doing what was right. He was doing God's will. She wanted to please God, too, but she wanted family…a complete family. She wanted to be close to her son. She wanted her son to be safe. Which would it be? Was Jesus her son, or should she be His disciple? At times, she must have wondered why she even had to make a choice. Why couldn't Jesus just come home? Why couldn't He serve God as a carpenter?

Some time later, Salome, the mother of James and John, two of Jesus' disciples, visited her. "Mary," she said, "I'm going to Jerusalem. I believe God is going to do something great with Jesus. I want James and John to be a part of that. I'm going with several other women from Galilee to Jerusalem. Why don't you go with us?"

Mary went, hoping perhaps to find some time alone with Jesus. Maybe if she talked with Him she could understand what was happening and get a grip on the future and her emotions. As it turned out, she would experience emotions deeper than any she ever felt before.

A Mother's Enduring Love

So many people were crowded into Jerusalem for Passover that Mary could not get near Jesus. The air was filled with tension, as if something ominous were going to take place, so Mary stayed close to the other Galilean women.

On Friday, as the women made their way to the Temple area, they saw everyone heading toward the edge of town, toward Golgotha.

"What is it? What's happening?" one of the women asked a fast walker.

"Haven't you heard? Jesus is being crucified."

Oh, no. Oh, no. Mary thought she would die on the spot. She could hardly breathe and would have fallen except that one of the other women caught her. Another one asked her if she needed to rest or wanted to return to the inn where they were staying. "No," she said, "I must go to Golgotha. I must be there for Him." She didn't understand Him, but He was her son and she loved Him.

They were raising the cross with Jesus nailed on it when the women arrived at the crucifixion scene. Mary stood there, looking on, seeing her son inflicted with pain and hearing Him ridiculed and reviled. As Herbert Lockyer says in his book, *All the Women of the Bible*, "Mary's deepest sword piercing came when in agony she stood beneath that old rugged cross and witnessed the degradation, desolation and death of the One whom she had brought into the world and intensely loved."

Mary's love endured, she *stood* by the cross, and Jesus saw her. As He looked down at her, He could not help but think of the days ahead and what they might be like for her. He wanted someone to protect her and look after her. His brothers don't appear to have been present, so He entrusted her to the care of the apostle John (John 19:27).

"Woman," He said tenderly to Mary, "behold, thy son!"

Then to John, His much-loved disciple, He said, "Behold, thy mother."

In the last moments of His life, and in the midst of pain and sorrow, He thought of His brokenhearted mother and arranged for her care. The gesture comforted Mary, closing the distance she felt. Her heart softened even more and—most importantly—her vision cleared. When she heard Jesus pray the prayer she had taught Him as a child, she yielded. As Jesus said, "Father, into Thy hands I commit My Spirit," Mary prayed, "Father, I surrender my Son to You. I am Your handmaiden, and I accept the life You have chosen for me."

Mary let go of Jesus as *her son* and accepted Him as *God's Son*. After Jesus' death and resurrection, she became one of Jesus' disciples. Perhaps she even encouraged His brothers to become disciples, too, because all of them gathered with Jesus' disciples and the Galilean women to prayerfully await the coming of the Holy Spirit (Acts 1:12–14).

Mary's life experiences help us understand what it means to be a Christ follower. It means responding to God in the good and bad times by submitting to God's will. Our response to His will, even when it is perplexing or painful, should be the same as hers: "I am the Lord's servant. Whatever God says, I accept."

chapter three

Anna:
A Christ Follower Worships Even When Her Heart Is Breaking

Luke 2:36–38

Have you noticed how many older people enjoy seeing a baby? If you take a baby to a nursing home, the faces of the residents light up. A friend of mine, June, included a real live baby in a nativity pageant at an assisted-living residence. As she arranged for the shepherds and the wise men, she thought how nice it would be to have a real live baby to be Jesus. Her husband made a manger and they filled it with straw. June laid some sheepskin on the hay for a comfy bed for the baby. The residents were enthralled as they watched the woman who played Mary lift the baby from the manger, hold her and pat her. Yes, a baby girl played Jesus!

After the pageant, as June gathered costumes and put away songbooks, she laid the baby back in the manger. The residents gathered around the manger and cooed over the baby. One resident reached down and touched the baby. As if on cue, the baby curled her little hand around the woman's bony finger; the resident was thrilled. She said, "Oh, honey, hasn't the Lord smiled on us today!"

Simeon, whom you met briefly in the story of Mary of Nazareth, and Anna must have had that same kind of joy—and more—when Mary and Joseph brought Jesus to the Temple. They were two old people who had waited a long time to see Jesus.

Faithfulness Rewarded

After Jesus was at least 41 days old, Mary and Joseph took Him to the Temple in Jerusalem for the ceremony of the Redemption of the Firstborn and for Mary's purification rite. William Barclay explains in *The Daily Study Bible* that, "According to the law (Exodus 13:2) every firstborn male, both of human beings and of cattle, belonged to God. That law may have been a recognition of the gracious power of God in giving human life. If it had been carried out literally life would have been disrupted. There was therefore a ceremony called the Redemption of the Firstborn (Numbers 18:16)." For the sum of five shekels, paid to the priests, parents could buy back their son from God.

When a woman had given birth, she was unclean for some time—if it was a boy for 40 days, if it was a girl for 80 days. She could manage her household and go about her daily business but she couldn't enter the Temple or take part in any religious ceremony (Leviticus 12). After her time of uncleanness was over, the new mother was to bring to the Temple a lamb for a burnt offering and a young pigeon for a sin offering; if she could not afford the lamb, she might bring another pigeon, as Mary did.

The mother was not required to take the offering to the Temple herself, but could send her offering by someone else. I'm sure Mary wanted to be there for Jesus' first visit to the Temple. The Redemption of the Firstborn wasn't just a ceremony to her; she wanted to dedicate her son to God. Plus, I would imagine there was also a little maternal pride involved. What new mother can resist showing off her baby! There were bound to be oohs and aahs, and sure enough, there were when Simeon and Anna saw Him.

Simeon and Anna were fixtures at the Temple. Simeon, a "just and devout" old man, was often there waiting "for the Consolation of Israel" (Luke 2:25 NKJV), meaning the fulfillment of Jewish messianic hopes. "The Holy Spirit was with him and had assured him that he would not die before he had seen the Lord's promised Messiah" (Luke 2:25–26). Ever since her husband died, just seven short years after they were married, Anna spent her days and nights worshiping God, fasting, and praying at the Temple.

When Simeon saw Jesus, God's Spirit revealed to him that baby Jesus was indeed the promised Messiah.

Simeon reached for Jesus, took Him in his arms, and thanked God. He exclaimed, "With my own eyes I have seen your salvation, which you have prepared in the presence of all peoples: A light to reveal your will to the Gentiles and bring glory to your people Israel" (Luke 2:30–32). Mary and Joseph were amazed at Simeon's words (Luke 2:33).

As Simeon was speaking, Anna walked up. She, too, recognized Jesus as the redemption of Jerusalem, which was no small feat considering the Jews weren't expecting the Messiah to be a baby. They associated the Messiah with riches, power, and worldly splendor. They were looking for a great champion like King David who would descend upon the earth and deliver them from the Romans and put them in charge.

In an instant, Anna recognized who Jesus was. There was no "let me think about it," or "I need to give this some consideration," or "I'll get back to you." Here was the Messiah in her arms as a baby, and she *knew* Him. How could that be? Simeon had a promise that he had clung to through the years, but the Bible doesn't say that Anna had such a promise. What enabled her to perceive who Jesus was?

Shaped by Worship

Anna's insight can be traced back to how she chose to handle sorrow. She had only been married seven short years when her husband died. While she didn't have a choice about what happened, she had a choice about her response.

Anna could have been very bitter about the devastating loss she experienced at such a young age; it is the kind of thing that could turn a person away from the Lord. She could have cried out in anguish over life's unfairness. *Why me? Why now?*

Sorrow can produce bitterness and resentment, but sorrow can also produce faith, peace, and purpose. Out of sorrow there can come serenity, graciousness, a steadfast faith, and a closeness to God that nothing else can bring *if* a woman chooses to give her sorrow to God. Anna did this. Piece by piece, she gave her broken heart to God.

When death ravaged her home, Anna made God's house her dwelling place. Night and day she was at the Temple. Herbert Lockyer puts it this way: "When as a young, motherless wife, God withdrew from her the earthly love she rejoiced in, she did not bury her hope in a grave" (from *All the Women of the Bible*). Rather she placed her hope in God.

She could have seethed over being left desolate with no one to care for her or to protect her, but instead she prayed and asked God for His help. She trusted God. She devoted herself to Him who had promised to be a husband to the widow (see Isaiah 54:4–5).

When she could have dwelt on her loss, she listened with sympathy as others talked about their losses and disappointment. She understood their concerns and responded by praying and fasting for them.

When she could have been overwhelmed by loneliness and haunted by memories of happier days, she interacted with those who came to the Temple. She was a prophetess who revealed God's will to them, and they put confidence in what she had to say.

Her age contributed to the well of wisdom out of which she shared. By the time she recognized baby Jesus, she was either eighty-four or had been a widow for eighty-four years. The Greek text is unclear, but either way, she had lived a long time. She made a choice about the years. As they stacked up, she could have resented them. As aging takes away the bloom and the strength of our bodies, it can take away zest for life and leave us feeling useless and unproductive. Cherished dreams die, and we become discontented and resigned to things as they are, unless we believe God has a purpose for us. Anna chose to respond to aging the same way she chose to respond to sorrow, by devoting herself to God. Anna's service at the Temple indicated she believed God had a purpose and place for her.

By the time Anna saw baby Jesus, she had spent most of her life in the house of the Lord. Therefore, when this first public appearance of the Messiah came to her attention, she was able to perceive who He was. Her spiritual sensitivity had been shaped by a lifetime of worship.

Life Shapers

As admirable as her devotion was, it was not a simple matter for Anna. If we look at the components of what shaped Anna's faith and devotion, you will see that it involved a continual turning toward Him. What does the Bible tell us about her?

She never ceased to worship. Throughout her long widowhood, Anna's devotion to Him was unswerving.

She never ceased to pray. She spent an unusual amount of time in prayer. The years had left Anna without bitterness and with an unshakable hope because she stayed in close contact with God every day. God was the source of her strength and prayer kept her close to that source.

She fasted. In spite of her age, she kept more than the customary fasts on Mondays and Thursdays. She fasted regularly, showing her self-sacrificing spirit and giving God a channel in which to speak to her.

She interacted with God's people. Anna prayed with people who came to the Temple and prophesied to them. Although women were excluded from the priesthood, some were prophetesses who participated in the ministry of the Word. In the Old Testament, women like Miriam (Moses' sister), Deborah (one of the judges), and Huldah (advisor to King Josiah) were called prophetesses. In the New Testament, the daughters of Philip (Acts 21:9) prophesied. These women were divinely inspired to make God's will known to others.

She learned. As she interacted with and listened to God's people as they came and went, she heard talk about the prophecies concerning the Messiah. Coming from a historic family, the daughter of Phanuel of the tribe of Asher, she was vitally interested in the signs of the times. She was so attuned to them that when she gazed on Jesus' face, Anna knew that past predictions were being fulfilled.

All of these components came together and solidified when Anna recognized baby Jesus as the promised Messiah. The natural response of this praying prophetess was to pray and to proclaim. She gave thanks to the Lord; her heart was full and overflowing as she sensed the significance of the moment. She proclaimed glad tidings to those who were also looking for the Messiah. Her years of faithful worship were rewarded when she was able to announce the birth of the Messiah to all who were looking for Him.

Anna's example is a good one for women because she chose to worship God even when her heart was breaking. That's a choice many women will be confronted with.

Women of Sorrow

By nature, most women are relationship oriented, and relationships change. Disruptions occur. Friends change or move away. Divorces happen. Loved ones die. Sometimes those relationships are so important to us that their loss feels like death itself.

Some women will experience the heartbreak of infertility; others lose a child or grieve over a child's behavior. Children can break our hearts so much that we instinctively understand Simeon's words to Mary: "Sorrow, like a sharp sword, will break your own heart" (Luke 2:35).

Sometimes the losses are intangible, but nevertheless painful. Dreams fail to materialize. Assumptions about life or about others are shattered.

At any one of these times it would be easy to become bitter, resentful, cynical, and hard, but Anna's example shows us another way—a way of serenity, peace, and purpose. It means taking the anguish and hurt of our sorrow and redirecting that energy toward pleasing God.

To follow her example doesn't mean we have to respond in exactly the same way Anna did. Later in this book, we'll see how another widow, Dorcas, handled her loss. It's the turning toward God and continually focusing on Him and His will that we want to emulate. How we turn isn't as important as the fact that we turn, as these two stories illustrate.

The April 2003 issue of *Missions Mosaic* magazine tells the story of Eileen Mullins, a woman who turned her tragedy to triumph by ministering to families of prisoners. Her son—who did not have even a traffic ticket on his record—murdered his wife while they were going through a bitter and difficult divorce. He was sentenced to 20 years in prison for manslaughter. Although deeply disappointed in her son's behavior, Eileen, a retired schoolteacher and the wife of a retired minister, visited him regularly in prison, making the long drive from her home to the prison.

On her frequent visits, she began to notice other visitors to the prison. There were poor single mothers bringing children to visit their fathers in prison. Many of them drove old, unreliable cars, and didn't even have money to buy snacks from the vending machines for their hungry children. Many of them had driven long distances to visit with their loved ones, and had to drive home the same night because they couldn't afford to stay in a motel.

Eileen's way of continually turning toward God was relying on His promise that "in all things God works for good" (Romans 8:28). This was her way of offering her sorrow to God, and God spoke to her in response. The

Lord told Eileen that she would have a ministry, and it would be called "Haven of Rest." She knew just as surely as Anna knew baby Jesus was the Messiah that she was to build a place for families to stay while visiting loved ones in prison, a haven where hurting families could rest and find shelter, food, and prayerful counsel, and that is what she has been doing ever since. She raises money, oversees the building, and directs the haven for hurting families.

Carole Bowgren watched her marriage unravel as she reached midlife. Her life had always been a fairly smooth one with no upheavals. Suddenly, she was facing divorce, and she found it devastating.

The divorce, when it came, was a total shock to Carole and to everyone else in her life. She and her husband had been active in church, and had even talked to young couples about how good marriage was and how to accept each other.

Carole turned to God. She started attending meetings of a Christian woman's organization. She said, "It was a place where I felt protected. My heart was so broken that first year. I needed all the support and encouragement I could get."

And like Anna, she began to pray. "I prayed for two things: that God would prevent bitterness from taking hold in me, and that I would be a quick learner, because the lessons were too painful to repeat." Soon she was rising each morning to pray for an hour. "Even though I was a Christian and read my Bible, I had never been in the habit of praying—not for my children, my marriage, or anything else," Carole recalled. "But I started to pray every day and began keeping a prayer list. Before long, my list grew and grew."

As Carole developed her prayer life, she found that emotional healing began. As she continued praying, she felt God preparing her to serve Him. She became involved in the women's organization that helped her. As she did, she felt like a flower beginning to blossom. Now she is a national representative with the group.

Like Anna, as God worked in her life, Carole was ready to proclaim. Carole said, "As I was going through this time of transition, God gave me this verse: 'Open your eyes and look at the fields! They are ripe for harvest' (John 4:35)." Now she is reaping the harvest by introducing women to a ministry that helps people come to know Christ, work she says is deeply rewarding. (The story of Carole Bowgren was told in the June/July 1999 issue of *Progress* magazine.)

If you respond this way, turning to God when your heart is broken, you will have a way to handle your heartbreak. You will indeed become a Christ follower. He, too, experienced grief and sorrow (Matthew 26:37). He said, "The sorrow in my heart is so great that it almost crushes me" (Matthew 26:38). Yet He prayerfully released those emotions to God so He could go ahead and do God's will. He prayed the prayer every Christ follower has to pray at sometime or another: "My Father…not what I want, but what you want" (Matthew 26:39).

chapter four

The Galilean Women:
Christ Followers
Give What They Have

Luke 8:1–3

What would you think if you saw this ad in a newspaper? "WANTED: Women with resources to invest in a revolutionary and to travel with him and his colleagues. Applicants must be tough, flexible, and courageous. Women concerned with immediate return on their investment need not apply."

If I saw an ad like that, I would think, *Who would have the gall to make such a request?* And, *What woman would be foolish enough to respond?*

As outrageous as the ad is, Jesus might have placed a similar one if there had been a *Galilean Gazette*. Right from the first, when He launched His ministry in Judea, Jesus asked people to accompany Him (John 1:35–51). His was not a solo ministry. This was especially true when His popularity mushroomed after He returned to Galilee. Wherever He went, crowds gathered around Him. Some were just curiosity seekers, others wanted their needs met, and some became His disciples. Out of this last group, Jesus chose a smaller group of twelve devoted followers to accompany Him. Called apostles, they traveled with Him through towns and villages as He preached the Good News about the Kingdom of God. Surprisingly, some Galilean women joined their entourage, supporting them and traveling with them (Luke 8:1–3).

I say "surprisingly," because if you were a woman in that day and time, you just didn't do this kind of thing. Ross Saunders, in his book *Outrageous Women, Outrageous God*, says that, "Women who traveled for other reasons than shopping and visiting relatives were always regarded with suspicion."

Tsk, Tsk, Tsk

On His way from Judea to Galilee, Jesus and several disciples stopped at a well in Samaria (read the story in John 4). Jesus was tired, so the disciples left Him there and went into town to get some food. When they returned, they were shocked to find Jesus talking with a woman who had come to draw water. Women were considered to be inferior to men, and good Jewish men didn't associate with them in public.

A rabbi might not even speak to his own wife or daughter or sister in public. If he did, it would be the end of his reputation. Some religious leaders were called the "bruised and bleeding Pharisees" because they shut their eyes when they saw a woman on the street. Consequently, they walked into walls and houses!

Contrary to established custom and accepted teaching, Jesus freely socialized with women. He talked openly with women without fearing criticism and without concern for His reputation.

Not only did Jesus socialize with women, He recognized their desire to learn and encouraged their interest. As a teacher, He didn't restrict His audiences, a position that differed radically from the usual Jewish attitude toward women. Jews did not encourage the full participation of women in religious life.

Only men and boys participated in the synagogue services. Many rabbis excluded women from their disciples. To them, women seemed incapable of studying the law. Many rabbis taught that it was better for the Law (Scriptures) to be burned than to fall into the hands of a woman. Women were allowed to take part in worship, but worship could only be celebrated if at least ten men were present. Women were not counted.

Jews weren't the only ones who restricted women. "In much of the first-century world, women were the property of men," Frank Stagg says in his book, *Studies in Luke's Gospel*. Women were accorded few legal rights and held a limited status. Generally, they could not own property or make tribal decisions. Their names were seldom listed in genealogical accounts. For the most part, men dominated in all power structures: civil, economic, military, and religious.

In this kind of limited environment, the idea of women traveling with men who were not their husbands was scandalous. Why were they not home looking after their families? Where did they sleep at night? What kind of relationships did they have with the men?

Jesus took a radical step when He included women as a part of His ministry team, but it was radical for the women, too. They went against culture to travel with Jesus. They showed independence and courage in adopting an unusual lifestyle. Who were these women, what did they give, and why did Jesus need them?

Who They Were

The Bible names three of the women: Mary, called Magdalene; Joanna, the wife of Chuza, Herod Antipas's steward; and Susanna. Only one of them is listed as "the wife of" someone, something that doesn't particularly strike us as significant, but it would have been to early Gospel readers. Ross Saunders explains, "In the Greco-Roman world of the time, women were never named in their own right. You will look in vain for the names of women in honorary inscriptions without also finding them named as the wife of, or the daughter of, or the sister of, or the mother of, some male person."

That Mary Magdalene and Susanna are listed without reference to a male sponsor may mean they were widows without brothers, fathers, or sons, or it could mean they were women of shame. According to Ross Saunders "if a woman was seen as an object of shame, then her husband or father or son was never named in association with her, since this would extend the shame to him."

Mary's or Susanna's shame could have been related to an illness or demon possession. The Bible says that the Galilean women who traveled with Jesus—and there were many more besides the three named—had been healed of "evil spirits and diseases" (Luke 8:2).

"Evil spirits and diseases" are such broad categories that it is hard to know exactly what kinds of ailments the women were healed from. It's doubtful that a regular type of illness such as having a fever would be shameful. Jesus healed a woman in Capernaum of a fever; she was associated with a male, Simon Peter, her son-in-law (Matthew 8:14–15; Mark 1:30–31; Luke 4:38–39).

More likely to be shameful would be the condition of the woman with the issue of blood (Matthew 9:20–22, Mark 5:25–34; Luke 8:43–48) whom Jesus healed. Any issue of blood meant that a woman was considered "defiled," rendering her unfit for social interaction.

Leprosy, too, was an illness of shame. Families disassociated themselves from leprous family members, leaving them to fend for themselves outside the community and to scavenge for food.

Various mental and emotional disturbances were ascribed to "demons," "evil spirits," or "unclean spirits." The behavior of those disturbed was weird and hard to understand. Frightened families distanced themselves from those affected.

Whether or not the women's being sick or demon-possessed explains their shame, it may explain why the

Galilean women overrode all fear of scandal to follow Jesus. When He healed them, Christ transformed their lives. Out of their gratitude, they were determined to follow Him, even in the face of public disapproval.

Jesus didn't need an ad in the *Galilean Gazette*. In who He was and in the way He treated women, Jesus displayed a HELP WANTED sign. Evelyn and Frank Stagg, in their book *Women in the World of Jesus*, state that these "women whose conditions were subject to scorn and penalty found in Jesus a liberator who not only enabled them to find health but who dignified them as full persons by accepting their own ministries to himself and the Twelve."

Consequently, the women willingly "used their own resources to help Jesus and his disciples" (Luke 8:3). What were those resources? What did they have to give? To some extent, we have to imagine.

What the Women Gave

I informally polled over sixty women and asked them what they thought the Galilean women would have contributed to Jesus' ministry. The majority answered that they imagined the women would have cooked meals, mended and washed clothes, washed dishes, and kept the camp organized!

Perhaps there is some truth in their answers, because the Bible says they "ministered unto him" (Luke 8:3 KJV).

The Greek for the verb *ministered* means literally "who were serving them." It comes from the Greek verb *diakoneo*, meaning "to serve." The verb form means to be an attendant, to wait upon menially as a servant, or to wait upon as a host, friend, or teacher. It is translated as ministering, helping, supporting, and serving. Angels ministered unto Jesus after His temptations (Matthew 4:11, Mark 1:13). Peter's mother-in-law ministered to Jesus and the others after Jesus healed her (Matthew 8:15, Mark 1:31, Luke 4:39).

The noun form is *diakonos*, from where we get the term "deacon." The term gradually gained a technical usage for a specific church office. Before that, at the time of the Galilean women, it was a general term used for anyone who served in any capacity. It could have meant an attendant, a waiter, a servant, a minister, or an errand-runner.

The main idea behind *diakonos* is practical service, so the resources the Galilean women had to give may very well have been their domestic abilities, but they could have had other resources. Luke 8:3 says they ministered to Jesus and the Twelve with "their substance" (KJV) or "their private means" (NASB). The Greek Luke used was *ta hyparchonta*, literally "those (things) belonging to someone," in the sense of possessions. The same expression is used in "sell your possessions, and give alms" (Luke 12:33 RSV), and "Truly, I say to you, he will set him over all his possessions" (Luke 12:44 RSV). Perhaps the Galilean women had financial resources to support Jesus' ministry. How could that be, since they lived in such a restrictive society?

Exceptions to the Rules

While women have often been held back in various ways throughout history, there have always been some women who defy the restrictions or do not fit the norm. They seem to be exceptions, people who do not fit society's cultural rules and expectations. Women were restricted financially in the first century, but it was also possible that some of them had access to wealth or earned money in some way. Here are some possibilities.

(1) Joanna is linked in the Bible with her husband, Chuza, who by his position was wealthy. As the steward of Herod Antipas, governor of Galilee, Chuza was the official who looked after his financial interests and his private property. He was the ruler of the house. He was the dispenser not only of the food, but of the money, and indeed, of everything that the household possessed. Perhaps Chuza was so grateful for Jesus' healing Joanna that he allowed her to go with Jesus and to use their wealth to support His ministry. Chuza owed his wife's restoration to Jesus. That she could go anywhere at all was due to Jesus.

(2) The exception to the custom of listing a woman with reference to a man, as mentioned above, applied to widows of famous and powerful people. Mary Magdalene and Susanna could have been widows who were independently wealthy.

(3) The Galilean women could have been property owners. Property ownership by women was not the

norm, but it did occur. Mosaic law provided for a daughter to inherit her father's land if he had no sons (see Numbers 27:1–11).

(4) The wealth of the Galilean women could have been from their own earnings. Proverbs 31 describes a woman who made linen garments and sold them for a profit (31:22, 24) and who invested in real estate (31:16). Lydia, whom we'll read about in chapter 10, traded in purple cloth. Priscilla, whose story we'll look at in chapter 12, was a tentmaker.

Even if the Galilean women weren't wealthy, I believe their gratitude was so great they would have found a way to support Jesus *and* the Twelve. The King James Version reads as if the support is for Jesus only ("unto him"), but most other versions say "for them," meaning Jesus and the Twelve. The better attested reading is "them." That would mean they gave a significant amount of support, but the Galilean women weren't easily deterred. If they had been, they wouldn't have risked their reputations to travel with Jesus. They were a determined group, not unlike mission-minded women in the late 1800s.

A Determined Spirit

When I read about the Galilean women, I was reminded of women in the late 1800s, another time when most women didn't earn or control much money. That didn't deter women from finding a way to support missions.

They "discovered that *regular* offerings of even a penny a week would eventually mount up," as historian Leon McBeth tells us in his book, *Women in Baptist Life*.

For example, in the Southern Baptist Convention, a denomination known for its extensive and effective stewardship program, the women of the mission societies taught and practiced tithing several years before the denomination generally accepted it. The women devised the plan whereby a person's offering was placed in an envelope and its purpose marked. There is no record of Baptist churches using offering envelopes before they learned it from the women.

Women also stressed the importance of regular giving each week, even if the amount was small. Instead of saving up one's offering until the amount became significant, they urged regular giving. McBeth argues that this was quite contrary to earlier Baptist practice, where churches often had only one or two offerings a year.

With little money of their own, they emphasized regular offerings, however small, and preferably given on Sunday. They distributed "mite boxes," containers for the offerings at home. A mite box was given to each woman, who placed at least two cents a week in the box. In ten years the Foreign Mission Board of the Southern Baptist Convention received $75,000 from mite box collections. On several occasions their gifts saved the mission boards from collapse.

More than the amount of money—which is impressive even by today's standards—there's a *spirit* here that we are talking about—a spirit evident in the Galilean

women and the missionary women. It is a spirit of determination. *If Jesus needs our help, we will find a way to
support Him.*

Wherever the Galilean women got their money,
whether it was a huge amount or a small one, they used
it to support Jesus and the Twelve. The Galilean women
were not parasites wanting to live off Him or groupies
wanting to bask in His fame. When they left their
homes to follow Jesus, they left to be supportive of Him
and the Twelve. Their support was invaluable because
Jesus needed them.

The Needs of Jesus

In one sense, Jesus was very rich. He said everything the
Father had was His (John 17:10). In another sense,
though, He wasn't rich at all. During His three years of
ministry, Jesus chose to live without a thing He could
call His own. When He was hungry, He came to a fig
tree by the roadside expecting to get His breakfast.
When He was tired, He borrowed a fishing boat to lie
down and sleep in. When He was thirsty, He asked the
woman at the well to give Him a drink of water. When
He wanted to teach a lesson about the bounds of eccle-
siastical and civil society, He said, "Bring me a coin."
Jesus depended on others for the donkey on which He
made His entry into Jerusalem. He borrowed the upper
room where He shared the Passover meal with the
Twelve and used the private garden of a friend for
prayer.

Although Jesus fed the multitudes by way of miracles,

the Bible doesn't tell us that He used His divine power to provide for His own physical needs. Even after Jesus fasted for forty days, Satan could not successfully tempt Jesus to turn stones into bread.

Because Jesus was poor and because He did not use supernatural power for His own needs, He needed the financial support—and the practical service—of the Galilean women.

The Galilean women may have used their financial resources to buy food, which they would then prepare for Jesus. When the touring group broke at night for camp, the Galilean women would glide back and forth through the tents, around the fires, here and there, doing those chores that cannot be ignored in any mode of life. Perhaps they carried a portable oven with them. Or perhaps they extemporized from a hole dug in the ground and inlaid with flat stones for baking bread and cooking stew. When fish were caught from the Sea of Galilee, they would need to be broiled. There would be earthenware jars or pots, firkins, dishes, and water bottles of goatskin to keep clean and to keep track of as they moved from place to place.

What an asset practical service would have been to Jesus! He had no place to lay His head. He remarked to a would-be disciple, "Foxes have holes, and birds have nests, but the Son of Man has no place to lie down and rest" (Luke 9:58).

I'm not implying that Jesus felt Himself above doing housekeeping jobs, but He had a busy, active ministry with people coming to Him at all hours. What a wonderful help it would have been for Him to have the support and practical service of the Galilean women. He needed help then, and He needs help now.

Help Is Still Wanted

When we think of being Christ followers, we mean women such as Elizabeth, Mary, and Anna who had hearts devoted to God's will, but that devotion also has a practical side. It means supporting Jesus' ongoing earthly ministry. The work of spreading the good news of the kingdom is ongoing, and Jesus still wants to bind wounds, heal the brokenhearted, and transform lives. Many people and many contributions are needed for His ministry to continue.

We may become leaders and innovators in doing His work, and we may be supportive assistants as the Galilean women were. Regardless, the story of the Galilean women reminds us that we all have something to give. We all have financial resources to give, even if it isn't a lot. Jesus praised the woman who gave two little copper coins (Luke 21:1–4, Mark 12:41–44). We can all do practical service. We can sweep floors, clean bathrooms, wash dishes, hammer nails, paint walls, cook, and more. We can never say, "There's nothing I can do." We all have resources to give; the question is, will we? Will we follow Christ as the Galilean women did?

chapter five

Mary Magdalene:
A Christ Follower
Has a Story to Share

Matthew 27:56, 61
Matthew 28:1–10
Mark 15:40, 47
Mark 16:1–11
Luke 8:1–3
Luke 24:10
John 19:25
John 20:1–18

As I pulled into the garage, Bob stuck his head out the door. As he reached for the grocery bags, he said, "Good news. Jerry just called. He, Judy, and the girls will be stopping by to spend the night on their way to Mexico. Won't it be good to see them?"

"Yeah, sure."

"What's the matter? You don't sound excited."

I wasn't, and that surprised me, because they were dear friends. Earlier, when we lived near them in Indiana, our families visited frequently with each other. Sometimes we would talk in the evenings on Jerry and Judy's big screened-in porch that ran across the entire width of their house. It was a restful place under tall shade trees that dotted their large, well-kept lawn. At other times, we gathered our children around the table in our kitchen, the biggest room in our little house.

As the time for their visit approached, my dread turned to agitation. Puzzled by my feelings, I shared my confusion with Julie at church on Wednesday evening before our company would arrive on Saturday. I said, "I don't understand why I feel the way I do. These are good friends."

Julie started questioning me. She began, "Are you ashamed of your house?"

"Funny you should ask. The truth is I have always admired Jerry and Judy's house—white, two-story house at the edge of town with lots of shade trees. When we lived near them, we lived in a small house in a subdivision with few trees. Our house now is bigger than the one back in the subdivision, but still modest in comparison with Judy and Jerry's. We have a few small trees now, but no grass! Still I'm not ashamed of our house."

"Are your friends picky eaters?" Julie continued.

"No, they love to eat. They have always been a joy to cook for, and we've had some great times over shared meals."

"Are they hard to get along with?"

"No, they are very congenial people, easy to be around, and their daughters are well-behaved and pleasant."

Not getting anywhere with her probing, Julie shrugged her shoulders and said, "Well, I'm just going to pray for you," and she did right then and there.

On the way home, as I was waiting for a traffic light to

change from red to green, God pulled back the curtains of my mind. He showed me that I had been envious of Jerry and Judy's house, and the way I had handled it was being secretly smug about my dynamic spiritual life. *They have a beautiful place to live, but I have exciting spiritual experiences.* Now I had to admit nothing spiritually exciting was happening. The last year, in fact, had been filled with spiritual disappointments. I had nothing in which I could take spiritual pride. *Aha, that's why I dread their coming. I don't have anything to brag about.*

When the light turned green, I turned to God. "Father," I prayed, "forgive me for the sin of spiritual pride. Take this sin out of my life and help me to be myself this weekend, a spiritual struggler, and nothing more."

By the time I reached home, the dread I felt about Judy and Jerry's coming was gone. I was not only ready to entertain company, but I felt as if all kinds of inner space had been freed up. Perhaps it had, for the sin of spiritual pride had been lodged in my heart for years, taking up valuable space, and now that inner space was swept clean, and it felt so good. When I think of how free I felt after confessing my sin, I couldn't help but wonder how Mary Magdalene must have felt to have experienced the removal of seven demons.

Seven What?

Mary Magdalene, one of the women who traveled with Jesus (the ones you met in the last chapter), was a woman identified by where she was from and by her demon possession.

To say "Mary Magdalene" makes it sounds like Magdalene is her middle name or a last name. It rolls off the tongue like Mary Elizabeth or Mary Franklin, but neither is the case. She's called Magdalene because she came from Magdala, a town located on the shores of the Sea of Galilee. Perhaps Jesus' group called her Mary Magdalene to distinguish her from the other Marys who also associated with them:

• Mary, the mother of James the younger (one of the apostles) and Joses (Mark 15:40)

• Mary, the wife of Clopas (John 19:25)

• Mary, Jesus' mother (John 19:25)

These three all had a male in their lives with whom their names—and honor—were associated, but Mary Magdalene may not have had that because she was possessed by demons. As we noted in the last chapter, the shame of demon possession often separated a person from her family.

It is no wonder that some families disassociated themselves from demon possessed relatives; their behavior was frightening and disturbing. When the Syro-Phoenician woman approached Jesus on behalf of her daughter who had an evil spirit (Matthew 15:22, Mark 7:25–26), she begged Jesus to drive out the demon. "'Son of David!' she cried out. 'Have mercy on me, sir! My daughter has a demon and is in a terrible condition'" (Matthew 15:22).

While the demon or demons reside within a person, the symptoms are visible externally. The symptoms may include:

• The inability to talk (Matthew 9:32–33, Mark 9:17).

Others afflicted screamed (Mark 1:26, 5:5), and some spoke audibly but strangely.

• Unusual strength. Nobody could keep the Gerasene demoniac tied with chains. "Many times his feet and his hands had been tied, but every time he broke the chains and smashed the irons on his feet. He was too strong for anyone to control him" (Mark 5:4).

• Strange behavior. The Gerasene demoniac "wandered among the tombs and through the hills, screaming and cutting himself with stones" (Mark 5:5). A boy possessed by an evil spirit foamed at the mouth, gritted his teeth, and became stiff all over (Mark 9:18).

• Violence. Two men who had demons in them were so fierce that no one dared travel the road by the caves they inhabited (Matthew 8:28).

• Blindness. "Then some people brought to Jesus a man who was blind and could not talk because he had a demon" (Matthew 12:22).

• Convulsions (Mark 1:26) and falling. A boy had such terrible attacks that he often fell in the fire or into water (Matthew 17:15).

In light of these symptoms, think how distraught and miserable Mary Magdalene must have been with seven demons (Luke 8:2). Seven demons could have referred literally to seven maladies, which Jesus cured all at one time or on seven separate occasions. Or, seven demons could have indicated a possession of more than ordinary magnitude or malignity. The Gerasene demoniac referred to himself as "Legion" or "Mob" because he had so many demons in him.

Either way, Mary would have been miserable as she contended with forces within (the actual residence of the evil spirits within) and without (dealing with her demon-controlled behavior and the responses of people towards her).

The evil spirits, taking up residence within Mary, robbed her of valuable inner space. As they fanned out within her, she may have even felt the pressure physically. And there were the voices of the demons always telling her what to do—things she didn't want to do. She was literally robbed of being the person God created her to be.

The forces that ravaged her soul also took their toll in other ways. Her family was ashamed of her. Her community regarded her as crazy. She was scorned, ridiculed, rebuked, and rebuffed.

The forces within and without threatened to destroy her, and Jesus came along and set her free. We are given no detailed account of Mary's encounter with Jesus when He set her free. How and when did she first meet Him? Did she hear about Him and seek His help as the Syro-Phoenician woman did for her daughter? Or did Jesus find her as He found the Gerasene demoniac and reach out to her in love? W. Hulitt Gloer says in his book, *As You Go*, that either way, Jesus "spoke of reconciliation, the reconciling of her life to the pattern of God's creative purpose for her life."

What freedom she must have experienced! Freedom from torment, freedom from fears, freedom from being controlled, and freedom to be herself. No wonder she left her regular life behind and spent her days following Christ and supporting His ministry.

After her deliverance, Mary became a devoted follower of Christ, as we saw in the last chapter, and some scholars say she became the leader of the Galilean women. Whenever this group is mentioned, Mary Magdalene is always named first. She was the forward one, the pacesetter, and an example for others to follow.

Maybe it was her natural ability as a leader that prompted Mary to eagerly run ahead of the other women and be the first at Jesus' tomb on Sunday morning following His death on Friday.

The First to See

The Galilean women followed Jesus from Galilee to Jerusalem. They were in the city when He was arrested and crucified. They stood by watching and comforting Jesus with their presence as He hung on the cross. Some of them went to Jesus' tomb early on Sunday morning, carrying the customary spices to anoint his body.

Mary Magdalene eagerly ran ahead and arrived first at the tomb. She found it opened. Alarmed, she immediately ran to tell Peter and John. Perhaps they could do something. She said, "They have taken the Lord from the tomb, and we don't know where they have put him!" (John 20:2).

Mary returned to the tomb and stood outside weeping.

"As she wept she stooped down and looked into the tomb. And she saw two angels in white sitting, one at the head and the other at the feet, where the body of Jesus had lain. Then they said to her, 'Woman, why are you weeping?'

"She said to them, 'Because they have taken away my Lord, and I do not know where they have laid Him.'

"Now when she had said this, she turned around and saw Jesus standing there, and did not know that it was Jesus. Jesus said to her, 'Woman, why are you weeping? Whom are you seeking?'

"She, supposing Him to be the gardener, said to Him, 'Sir, if You have carried Him away, tell me where You have laid Him, and I will take Him away.'

"Jesus said to her, 'Mary!'

"She turned and said to Him, 'Rabboni!' (which is to say, Teacher)."
—John 20:11–16 NKJV

Oh, it was Jesus! She wanted to reach out and touch Him, grab hold of Him, but Jesus said, "Do not hold on to me....But go to my brothers and tell them that I am returning to him who is my Father and their Father, my God and their God" (John 20:17), and go she did. She returned to the small band of bewildered disciples and said, "I have seen the Lord!" Mary Magdalene had a story to tell.

Make That "Stories"

Mary was valuable to Jesus' ministry with her financial contributions, her practical service, and her leadership skills, but she also had something else to offer—stories.

After her deliverance from demon possession, she could share with people in the crowds that surrounded Jesus, "I want to encourage you to bring your sick and your demon possessed to Jesus because He healed me. You wouldn't believe what a tormented life I had, but Jesus changed all that when He set me free."

When she returned to Magdala and people noted her serenity in contrast to the tormented woman she was when she left, she could say, "I have been with Jesus."

After the resurrection, she could tell people how hopeless she felt when Jesus was on the cross and how her grief was so intense. "But you won't believe what happened. Jesus appeared. Yes, that's right. I thought He was dead. I watched His crucifixion. I saw the soldiers pierce His side. He was really dead. I watched them put Him in the tomb. But He came back to life. He stood before me; He called my name. I tell you, I'll never be the same again."

Every Christian has stories to tell, just as Mary did.

Stories to Tell

Being Christ followers implies we have stories to tell because our lives have been transformed. The initial transformation occurred when we became believers. We were living life without Christ, and then we encountered Christ, became believers, and began a life with Christ.

We also have resurrection stories that take place in our

lives, when we were in what we deemed a hopeless situation, and Christ presented Himself in such a way that hope surged through us.

We also have stories that evolve out of our relationship with Him or as we serve Him. We may have testimonies about the benefits of a quiet time, of participating in Bible study, of memorizing Scriptures, of tithing, and of witnessing. Testimonies may be about struggle and renewal, about new insights gained, and about forgiveness of sin, like my story of when I was convicted of the sin of spiritual pride.

For some, the transformation experiences may be quiet and low key, as mine was when I prayed at the stoplight. For others, the experience may be emotional, as I imagine Mary Magdalene's experiences were. For some, the experience may be very dramatic, as it was for the apostle Paul.

Paul was heading to Damascus from Jerusalem to arrest Christians because they were followers of Jesus. A bright light blinded him, and the resurrected Christ appeared to him. This experience convinced Paul that Jesus was God's Son, and Paul's life was completely redirected by this experience. Instead of arresting Christians, he became a leader of Christians.

In most of the stories that Christ followers have, there is a *before* and an *after*. The *before* refers to one's previous condition, and the *after* contrasts with it. The degree of contrast may be greater for some experiences than for others. The degree is not what matters. What matters is the certainty—certainty like the blind man whom Jesus healed. When the Pharisees questioned him, he said, "One thing I do know: I was blind, and now I see" (John 9:25). He *knew* what happened to him.

You'll need this certainty because not everyone will believe you when you tell your stories. As exciting as Mary's story of seeing the resurrected Jesus was, when she went and told His disciples, they were mourning and weeping and "when they heard her say that Jesus was alive and that she had seen him, they did not believe her" (Mark 16:11). Part of the reason they did not believe may have been the incredibility of what she was saying—*The man I saw die is now alive. Impossible!*

Another reason may be that she was a woman. According to the famous Jewish historian, Josephus, women were not competent to witness. When Paul listed the witnesses to Jesus' resurrection (1 Corinthians 15:2–7), he did not include Mary Magdalene's name. Women were not considered credible witnesses.

When we share our stories of Christ's transformation in our lives, whether it was major or minor, we may receive disinterested looks or arched eyebrows that question. Listeners may say, "Uh, yeah, sure, that's nice," "That's interesting," or "I'm glad for you," but that doesn't negate the value of having a story to tell.

The Value of Stories

Some listeners will believe our stories. Jesus assured us through His story about sowing seed—which is what we do when we tell our stories—that a harvest will occur (Matthew 13:1–8). Not all seeds will take root, sprout, and grow, but some will. Our stories will help unbelievers find Christ and encourage Christians when they are going through difficult times.

Telling the story will help us, too. It is rejuvenating to share our story with others. It fans the flame within us as we recall how God has worked in our lives (2 Timothy 1:6).

Having a story also humbles us. Because we know the *before* as well as the *after*, we can identify with others and their needs. When Jerry and Judy came to visit, we lounged in the living room after a nice meal together. The children busied themselves in the family room. As we talked, Judy admitted that she was struggling with a perplexing spiritual question. The four of us spent most of the evening discussing it. As we talked we experienced the fellowship of sharing when we truly felt like brothers and sisters in Christ. Later, after they returned to Indiana from Mexico, Judy wrote to say that their evening with us was the best part of the trip.

I can imagine how it might have been otherwise if God had not convicted me of my spiritual pride earlier in the week. What glib answers I might have given Judy's question! As it was, I didn't have *the* answer to Judy's question, but I could struggle along with her and encourage her because I was also a spiritual struggler—something I wouldn't have acknowledged if I hadn't been convicted— and freed—of spiritual pride.

chapter six

Martha of Bethany:
A Christ Follower Cares about the Details

Luke 10:38–42
John 11:1–44
John 12:1–8

The time is 5:55 on a Wednesday evening. From the church parking lot, families are heading toward the door to the church's fellowship hall. Fathers are hurrying children along, and mothers are carrying casseroles and salads. They are looking forward to this monthly meal—they only had to fix one dish instead of several, and no clean up afterwards. Dads are hungry, and the children excited about playing with their friends. But as they enter the fellowship hall, they find it almost dark with only a fluorescent emergency light on. There are no tablecloths on the table, no drinks fixed, no rolls warming in the oven, no plates or silverware waiting. Puzzled, the adults turn and look at each other. *What's going on?*

Chad and Berry, college students and brothers, catch a ride home for Christmas. The driver questions the brothers about Christmas, but the guys act detached, as if Christmas doesn't really matter—it's kid stuff. But as the conversation winds down, Chad daydreams about Mom's Christmas cookies and her homemade soup. *It will be so good to get a break from fast food.* On the other side of the car, Berry is having his own dreams of a nicely decorated house, a fire in the fireplace, and lots of presents under the tree. He smiles to himself, *Maybe I haven't outgrown Christmas as much as I thought!* When they arrive home, they snatch their luggage, say good-bye, and head for the house. When they open the door, they don't see any signs of Christmas except for the traditional nativity scene on the mantle. Their mother greets them, they chat, and then she says, "Let's go out for pizza."

"But we thought…well, we eat a lot of pizza at school."

"I'm sorry, guys, I didn't have time to make soup. I could try to whip up something, but there's really not anything here to work with. I haven't been grocery shopping for a while. Besides, I want to talk to you. It's about the gifts…I thought we would skip them this year."

It's midmorning and Anne is sitting with a notepad and chewing on her pencil as she plans next week's menus. The phone rings, breaking the silence. Her mother has been injured in an automobile accident. She is needed right away. Anne packs a few things, calls her husband at work, and heads for her mother's. As she's driving down the highway, she thinks about her abrupt departure. She hopes Don, her husband, will look at the menus posted on the refrigerator and see what to fix for the girls' supper. She also hopes he remembers to take their daughter Linda to her band concert that night. It's on the calendar. He'll surely glance at the calendar.

That evening, Don looks in the fridge, but doesn't see anything to eat, so he fixes the girls peanut butter and jelly sandwiches. Afterwards, Linda goes to her room to read, Sarah goes outside to play, and Don heads to the basement to work. He runs out of glue, so he heads to Wal-Mart. Sarah comes inside when it starts getting dark. She sees the only light on in the house is in Linda's room. She knocks on the door and says, "Hey, didn't you have a band program tonight?"

Linda jumps up. "Oh, yeah, I did. Hey, it's already started. Where's Dad? I'll need a ride."

"I think he's gone. I didn't see anybody when I came in."

"Oh, no. I was supposed to get an award tonight."

These three scenarios give you an idea of what this world would be like without people who look after the details of life. In other words, what this world would be like without Marthas.

I've long felt that Martha of Mary-and-Martha fame gets a bad rap. She was a Christ follower who exhibited strong faith, yet she is often only remembered for her outburst when she wanted her sister, Mary, to help with dinner.

When Jesus Came to Dinner

If Martha were filling out an income tax form, she would check "head of household." Her brother, Lazarus, and sister, Mary, lived with Martha in her home in Bethany, about two miles from Jerusalem.

Jesus, with some of His disciples, was on His way to Jerusalem when "Martha received him into her house" (Luke 10:38 KJV). The Greek word used for "received" here is an ancient word used for welcoming a guest or visitor."

Did Jesus just show up and knock on Martha's door? According to some Bible scholars, it might have happened that way. The possibility is strong that a long-term friendship existed between Jesus and Martha, Mary, and Lazarus (see John 11:5), so He could have gone directly to Martha's house when He got to Bethany, knowing she would welcome Him. Her door was always open.

Or did some of Jesus' disciples arrange for the visit when they were in the area? Earlier Jesus had sent out seventy disciples into the villages and towns of Judea. Perhaps some of them told Martha about Jesus, adding to the stories she already heard. She was intrigued, so she told the disciples, "The next time Jesus is in Bethany on His way to Jerusalem, plan on His coming to my house."

Or perhaps it was a spontaneous invitation. Maybe

Martha was in the market buying meat for dinner when she heard a commotion. A crowd was coming down the street. Their focus was on the man in the center. He was talking. Martha put down what she was looking at and went to see who the man was. It was Jesus, the Nazarene, the one whom many were saying was the Messiah. She wanted to know more. It was nervy of her, but when she got a chance, she invited Jesus to her home.

However it may have developed, Martha was in charge.

Guest Stress

Martha wasn't forced to entertain Jesus. She welcomed Him in her home. But even when you want to entertain, there's often stress associated with it, especially if it is someone you would really like to please. Among Jews, showing hospitality to a traveling teacher was a special privilege. Recognizing the importance of the occasion and Jesus' celebrity status, Martha wanted to do her best. She wanted to please Him, so she began fixing lots of food, fluffing the cushions, looking for serving pieces, and finding a place for everyone to sit.

How many people was Martha actually serving? Did she entertain Jesus or were some disciples part of the group, too? If the disciples were present, the numbers must have intensified the pressure Martha felt.

No one stepped forward to help Martha. Where was Lazarus? And where was Mary? Just when Martha really needed her sister, she was sitting at Jesus' feet, listening to Him teach (Luke 10:39). Why was she not helping?

As we picture this scene, it would be easy to assume that Mary and Jesus were in the living room relaxing while Martha was stewing over a hot stove in the kitchen, but we cannot be sure. Many Judean houses consisted of only one room, which served as living room, dining room, and bedroom. If this were the case, Martha would have had the frustration of trying to concentrate with people around her and teaching going on, teaching that she would have liked to have been a part of. As beads of perspiration popped out on her forehead, thoughts of all *she* was responsible for started rolling around in her head. She became "cumbered about much serving" (Luke 10:40 KJV). Finally, she couldn't stand it any longer.

Martha said to Jesus, "Lord, don't you care that my sister has left me to do all the work by myself? Tell her to come and help me!" (Luke 10:40).

Do you find it strange that Martha went to Jesus instead of Mary? Why didn't she just say, "Mary, can I see you for a minute outside?" And then out of the ears of her guest, and in a way that wouldn't embarrass Mary, she could have said, "Look, Mary, I'm your sister and I need your help. If you help me, we can get the meal served, and then we can both get to listen to Jesus."

Well, sure, that would have been the rational, thought-out-ahead response to make, but when we are agitated, frustrated, and sweaty it is hard to think things through and do the right thing. Martha, in the heat of the moment, simply erupted. I know because I have done the same thing.

Lord, Don't You Care?

Once I erupted at some students from my Sunday school class of single young adults. My co-teacher and I truly felt like Marthas as we looked after the details of having an ongoing ministry with this age group. We worked at it as if we were paid professionals instead of volunteers, planning parties, retreats, and outings. All the time we were providing them a place for learning and for meeting their friends, I often suspected they cared more for the friend part than the learning. Nevertheless, we persevered and lived in the hope that the students would eventually want to be faithful to the Sunday morning class and to studying God's Word. We really needed their presence on Sunday morning. If a new person came, and there were only one or two students there, then likely he would not come back. We needed commitment if the class were to grow.

One morning, after a well-prepared lesson and only two students there to participate, I walked into the sanctuary to see several members who had not been present for class laughing and talking. Visibly angry, I interrupted them, "Where were you this morning? You made it for the worship service. Why couldn't you make it for Sunday school?"

Needless to say, I did not encourage loyalty or commitment when I spoke this way! It was a long, long time, plus apologies on my part, before they returned to the group activities; I don't think they ever returned to Sunday school.

When I erupted at the students, I was really asking Martha's question: "Lord, don't You care? Why don't

You bless my efforts? I'm trying so hard to do this right, but yet my class never grows. Am I not pleasing You?" When our efforts as Christ followers don't show any progress or fruit, when we get discouraged, we may be tempted to cry, "God, don't You care?"

Even if you don't verbally erupt as Martha and I did, you may still have similar rumblings rolling around in your mind. *What about me, God? Why won't You bless what I am doing?* When we sincerely ask God if He cares, we usually receive reassurance, but sometimes we receive more. We may receive a lesson as Martha did.

Jesus' Reply

To her outburst, Jesus affectionately replied, "Martha, Martha," and validated her feelings: "You are worried and troubled over so many things" (Luke 10:41). He had been paying attention; what she was experiencing had not gone unnoticed. He was not indifferent to Martha's needs, yet in the situation He could only reprove her. Those "many things"—those details—had gotten the best of Martha. In contrast, He said, "Just one is needed. Mary has chosen the right thing, and it will not be taken away from her" (Luke 10:42).

In Martha's home, Jesus must have hoped for a quiet retreat from hustle, bustle, and activity. What good entertaining would have meant to Him at this point was quiet relaxation with maybe a sandwich or a cup of water instead of abundance of food and a frenzied host. In her anxiety to serve Him *in her way*, Martha was forcing on Him the very things He wanted to escape. She wanted to do too much in making the visit special for Jesus and missed sensing what would have really pleased Him. A simpler meal and some time together would have sufficed.

Even with the best of intentions, it is easy for many of us who look after details of life to go into overdrive and miss what is most important. We work so hard on elaborate decorations to make an outreach event special that we are too exhausted to extend personal invitations to the women we are trying to reach. Or we work so hard taking care of all holiday details that Christmas comes and goes without us experiencing any spiritual meaning. We enroll our children in so many activities that we never have time to just "be" with our children, to enjoy them as the precious children they are.

Jesus' rebuke of Martha is not to imply that practical service is unimportant. Martha's service was important. Her home provided a place for her Mary and Lazarus to live, and a place for Jesus to stay. Her invitation provided a place for Mary to learn at Jesus' feet. On other occasions, Jesus had much to say about practical service, and the Bible has much to say about hospitality. The Marthas among us look after the details and hold the world together.

Rather, Jesus' rebuke was a call for understanding and balance. Even Mary's approach could use some balance. I have often wondered why Mary didn't say, "Jesus, ask Martha to come in here and listen; she needs to hear this." Mary wouldn't have had the chance to sit at Jesus' feet if Martha hadn't invited Jesus to her home. We all need Marthas in our lives, and we need to be respectful to them and grateful for them.

Martha's story shows us that she was a responsible woman, a leader capable of looking after many details and looking after the needs of others. She also must have been a quick learner. The lesson Jesus taught her must have prompted her to give more attention to spiritual things, because the next time we see her, we learn that she is a woman of incredible faith.

The Great Confession

Leaving Martha's house, Jesus went on to Jerusalem, then into the countryside of Judea. Because of the increasing hostility of the Jews, Jesus and the disciples transferred their ministry to the region of Perea, where John had baptized people in the past. While Jesus was there, Mary and Martha sent Him a message about Lazarus: "Lord, the one you love is sick" (John 11:3 NIV).

Jesus replied, "The final result of this sickness will not be the death of Lazarus; this has happened in order to bring glory to God, and it will be the means by which the Son of God will receive glory" (John 11:4).

The next few days must have challenged Martha's faith, for in spite of what Jesus said, Lazarus died. Was Jesus wrong? It must have seemed that way to her. What else could she think? If Jesus had been wrong about this, how could she be sure He was right about other things? How could she trust His teaching?"

We could hardly blame Martha if she felt this way, but when Jesus arrived in Bethany a few days later, He found her faith and trust alive. Hearing that Jesus was coming, Martha, ever the leader and protector, rushed out to greet Him, giving Mary time to grieve with her friends in the house.

Never hesitant to speak her mind, Martha said, "Lord, if you had been here, my brother would not have died" (John 11:21 NIV). Martha knew that Jesus had already shown His power over death (John 4:46–54). She knew He had the power to give life and she recognized that God was still at work in Jesus. She said, "But I know that even now God will give you whatever you ask him for" (John 11:22).

"Jesus said to her, 'Your brother will rise again.' Martha answered, 'I know he will rise again in the resurrection at the last day'" (John 11:23–24 NIV).

In response to her expressions of faith, Jesus made an astounding claim: "I am the resurrection and the life. He who believes in me will live, even though he dies; and whoever lives and believes in me will never die" (John 11:25–26 NIV).

Jesus' claim was incredible—almost unbelievable. Yet when He said to Martha, "Do you believe this?" (John 11:26), she responded with the most dramatic confession up to this point in John's Gospel. She said, "Yes, Lord, I believe that You are the Christ, the Son of God, who is to come into the world" (John 11:27 NKJV)

The significance of her statement becomes apparent when we remember Peter's confession of faith at Caesarea Philippi. When Jesus asked His disciples, "Who do you say I am?" Peter answered, "You are the Christ, the Son of the living God" (Matthew 16:16

NKJV; see also Mark 8:29).

In Mark's Gospel, Peter's statement is the primary confession of faith and the pivotal point in the narrative. In John (whose narrative does not contain Peter's confession), Martha makes the primary confession of faith. W. Hulitt Gloer says in his book, *As You Go*, "As Peter's confession stands as the pivotal midpoint in Mark, so Martha's confession stands at the climactic midpoint in John. Thus, in John's Gospel, the proclamation of Jesus' identity is made by Martha. Hers is an incredible confession that affirms an incredible claim."

As remarkable as her faith is, though, Martha doesn't stop being Martha. She remains a woman concerned about people and the details of life. After Martha's conversation with Jesus, she thought of Mary. She returned to the house and told her, "The Teacher is here and is asking for you" (John 11:28).

When Jesus, along with Martha and Mary and others, went to Lazarus' tomb, He commanded the men to roll back the stone over the mouth of the cave. Martha was aware of one of those details others were overlooking. She protested, "There will be a bad smell, Lord. He has been buried four days!" (John 11:39).

Later, at a celebration to honor Jesus, Martha helped serve the meal (John 12:2). Martha's serving provided Mary with another structured environment in which she could focus on Jesus, which she did by anointing Him with a very precious ointment and wiping His feet with her hair (John 12:3–8).

That's Martha! Always thinking of others. Always noting the details. Always serving. But now as you look at her, I hope you also see a woman of faith. Jesus might have reproved her at one point, but at another one, He honored her by revealing His nature: "I am the resurrection and the life." Now do you see why I say there's more to Martha than one emotional outburst? She was a Christ follower with a strong faith, who lived it out in a practical, detailed way.

chapter seven

Mary of Bethany:
A Christ Follower Is Sensitive

Luke 10:38–42
John 11:1–46
John 12:1–8
Matthew 26:6–13
Mark 14:3–9

Sometimes I think God created women with special antennae that are ever moving and circulating, picking up all sorts of information and making interpretations about what they collect. Oh, these antennae are not visible to the naked eye, but they are there, receiving information and responding to stimuli around them.

With their antennae, women pick up significant information from the tone of a person's voice or intensity of one's expression. They are also able to interpret social cues such as posture and gesture. They can sense differences between what people say and what they mean, and they pick up nuances that reveal another person's true feelings.

As women receive this information, internal responses are triggered. They unscramble and interpret the verbal and nonverbal information they collect. They decide on appropriate courses of action—the best way to respond to what they have learned. They are perceptive about what needs to be done and sympathetic to the individuals involved.

Some women are more sensitive than others. Mary of Bethany, Martha's sister, must have been a very sensitive woman. She picked up on information around her that others missed. She sensed what Jesus really needed and wanted when others were oblivious. She doesn't say much about what she observes, but her actions reflect her sensitive spirit. If she kept a journal, here is what I imagine she might have written.

Journal Entry

Jesus came to our house today. As He entered the door I noticed He appeared tired and weary, although He enthusiastically greeted Martha, Lazarus, and me. I looked for a chance to ask Him how He was doing, but it wasn't easy with the disciples milling around and Martha hustling and bustling to put together one of her bountiful meals. Finally there was a lull in the conversation, and I asked Him what He had been doing.

"I have been answering people's questions and helping them with their dilemmas. I've also been trying to train the disciples."

"How's that going?" I asked.

"Well, it's been hard to find places for training where people will leave us alone so I can teach without interruption. I'm concerned the disciples aren't really catching on. They're distracted…" His voice kind of trailed off, and He looked off into the distance. "They just don't seem to realize time is running out."

Martha was preparing a banquet, bless her, but I had to wonder if that was what He really wanted. Quiet, unhurriedness, and a good listener—a listener who really tried to understand—seemed to me to be more what He needed, so I planted myself at His feet and listened. I gave Him my undivided attention.

I was so engrossed in what Jesus was saying that I failed to help Martha. I even forgot that women usually didn't get to experience this kind of thing—being taught by a rabbi. A part of me knew it was scandalous behavior, but Jesus didn't discourage me. In fact, my presence seemed to bless Him. When Martha said she needed my help, Jesus said, "Leave her alone, for she has chosen the best thing," and indeed I had.

Journal Entry

Lazarus, my dear brother, died today. The pain of the loss is almost unbearable. What will Martha and I do without him?

And the really sad thing is he probably wouldn't have died if Jesus had been here. He's over in Perea right now trying to escape the enemies who pursued Him so relentlessly in Judea. When Lazarus got sick, Martha and I sent a messenger to tell Jesus, and we were certain that He would come quickly when He found out, but He didn't. I know Jesus is busy and that His work is important, but still I thought He would come back right away. I know He loves Lazarus, Martha, and me, but I don't understand why He didn't return to help us. It just breaks my heart, and it makes me angry. He healed others; why wouldn't He heal Lazarus?

Journal Entry

Jesus finally came back today, four days after Lazarus was buried. I confess I didn't have the heart to go meet Him. I was just so distraught over losing Lazarus and so disappointed in Jesus for not coming sooner. Many of our friends and neighbors had gathered around Martha and me to comfort us and to share our grief. When Martha, my strong sister with her direct ways, heard that Jesus was coming, she went outside the village to meet Jesus, but I stayed in the house. Martha and Jesus talked for a while and then she came back to the house and whispered in my ear, "Jesus is here, and He is asking for you."

I thought, *Jesus wants to see me. Maybe He is concerned about me. Maybe He really does care.*

Still weeping—the tears have flowed profusely since Lazarus died—I went to meet Him. Those who came to comfort us followed. They thought I was going to Lazarus' tomb. We did end up there, but first I had to let Jesus know how disappointed I was. When I saw Him, I fell at His feet: "Lord, if you had been here, my brother would not have died!" (John 11:32). There was still plenty of anger with me.

Jesus saw us all weeping, and He started weeping, too. I had never seen Jesus cry before, and I'll admit my heart softened and my anger melted. To think that Jesus, with all He had going on, with all the people He saw and interacted with day after day, sensed what we were feeling and joined right in…well, that just touched my heart so much. I didn't have a doubt any longer about His love for Lazarus. My anger was gone, but then some of our friends said loud enough for Jesus to hear, "He gave sight to the blind man, didn't he? Could he not have kept Lazarus from dying?" (John 11:37).

I could tell by the way Jesus clenched His jaw that He was deeply moved again. As He headed for Lazarus' tomb, we all followed, and right there before our eyes, Jesus prayed and ordered Lazarus out of the tomb. And Lazarus came out! What a sight! What a moment! I laughed and laughed. I was so happy.

I'll never forget this day. As I write this, our home is peaceful once again with Lazarus back home sleeping in his own bed. I wonder about Jesus, though. He's back on the road again, which was probably a good thing. Some of our guests were upset by what Jesus did and reported Him to the Sanhedrin.

Journal Entry

Lazarus said Jesus has gone to Ephraim. I think it was a wise move. From what I overhear when I go to the market, Jesus' raising Lazarus from the dead rankled the Jewish authorities in Jerusalem. Some even say they want to kill

Jesus. I hope that isn't true. Oh, I just can't bear the thought.

Passover is near, and everyone is wondering, will Jesus come? That's the question on the minds of everyone. In the marketplace, I heard people talking and speculating. Some say He won't come. Others say He will. My feelings are mixed. I think it is dangerous for Him to return, but I would like very much to see Him again and to learn more from Him.

Journal Entry

Lazarus wasn't the only one in Bethany healed by Jesus. Simon, a leper, was healed, too. Simon suggested we have a celebration at his place if Jesus comes back from Ephraim for the Passover. He asked Lazarus, Martha, and me to help him, and we began making plans. It was a good thing because Jesus came back today.

Martha and I hurried into town to buy fresh meat for the banquet meal. As Martha was inspecting the poultry, I heard people saying things like, "We'll get that Nazarene no matter what it takes," and "Let's do it while many people are in town for the Passover. That way, we won't get caught." Fear for Jesus leaped up in my throat, even though I know Jesus can do many mighty miracles, even call on God's angels to protect Him; but these men had such mean, determined looks on their faces.

I had hoped for a chance to talk with Jesus alone at Simon's, but there were too many people around. The disciples were there, plus curious people lining the walls, wanting to watch the party and hear what Jesus said.

Finally, Simon, Lazarus, Jesus, and the disciples—the honored guests—sat down at the table. The disciples were giddy with excitement; they were certain this banquet would usher in Jesus' messianic kingdom. They seemed unaware of impending doom.

I felt it, though. I looked at Jesus and thought, *I wish there were some way I could show Him how much He means to me and that I understand what is happening, but too many people surround him.* I started to let it go when it struck me, *What if this is my last chance to do something special for Him?* As I thought about this, I fiddled with the phial of perfume I wore around my neck. Simultaneously I noticed that no one was attending to Jesus' needs, washing his feet and anointing His head with oil—something hosts usually do for honored guests.

I wanted to do that for Jesus, but I wondered how could I get to Him. And what would I use? I had no bowl or towel with me.

Then it occurred to me that my perfume might work. At first I hesitated at the idea. My perfume cost so much— nearly a year's wage for a working man. But this was Jesus. I wanted to do something for Him then, before it was too late. While Martha served, I wedged my way around the guests who had their feet stretched out behind them as they reclined at the table. When I was behind Jesus, I reached as far as I could and touched Jesus' forehead with the perfume. He looked at me then, and His eyes were so appreciative that I poured the rest of the perfume on His feet. I don't think many noticed what I was doing until the sweet smell of the perfume filled the place. Then everyone looked at me, and by then, I had let down my long hair so

I would have something to wipe Jesus' feet dry.

That's when Judas and some of the others started criticizing me. They said the perfume should have been sold and the money given to the poor. Maybe it was an extravagant thing to do, but I would do it again because I think I pleased Jesus. To the critics He said, "Let her alone. She's done a fine and beautiful thing. She has prepared my body ahead of time for burial."

From Mary's journal entries, you can see that Mary was a Christ follower with sensitivity and insight. She picked up significant information around her. She sensed Jesus' feelings and how to please Him. She had the foresight to recognize impending developments before they fully materialized and became obvious to others. Why didn't Martha, Judas and the disciples see what Mary saw?

Sensitivity Blockers

While I mentioned above that women as a whole seem to be more sensitive than men, that doesn't mean men aren't sensitive. All of us possess this trait to some degree. We are all born with sensitivity, but its effectiveness can be diminished by many things, such as the way we were raised, the way we were taught, work responsibilities, painful experiences, rigid thought patterns, and even sin.

Martha and Mary weren't equally sensitive, but you can't say Martha lacked sensitivity. She was sensitive to people who needed friends, food, and a place to "hang out." She was sensitive to Mary's needs when she was grieving. But her earnestness "to do" may have diminished her sensitivity. Sometimes we get bent on doing something a certain way, and we think it always has to be that way. Martha may have thought that the way to entertain is always with lots of food, whereas a more sensitive person would know that some occasions call for a banquet and others call for a sandwich. Or Martha's sensitivity could have been blocked by her anxiety over entertaining. One of the things Jesus told Martha was, "You are worried and troubled over so many things" (Luke 10:41).

Judas' selfishness interfered with his being sensitive. He tried to camouflage his selfishness as concern for the poor. After Mary poured out the perfume on Jesus' feet, Judas said, "Why wasn't this perfume sold for three hundred silver coins and the money given to the poor?" (John 12:5). Judas attempted to contrast Mary's waste with the good that could have been done with the ointment. It could have been sold and the proceeds used to alleviate the needs of the poor, of which there were many in Judea; but those were pseudo-concerns. Judas's real reason for objecting to Mary's wasteful act lay in the fact that he wanted the money to be placed in the common treasury of the disciples (John 12:6). As treasurer of the twelve, Judas carried the moneybag and from time to time would help himself to the money.

But Judas wasn't the only one who criticized Mary's wastefulness. Others voiced similar grievances (Mark 14:4), and the disciples were among them (Matthew 26:8). Jesus explained to them that Mary poured perfume on His body to prepare it for burial (Mark 14:8). The disciples spent more time with Jesus than anyone. Shouldn't they have sensed His death was near? Yes, they should have, but their minds were elsewhere.

When Jesus began teaching the disciples that He must suffer and die, Peter would not hear of it (Mark 8:31–33). When Jesus spoke of His death a second time, the disciples discussed their relative positions in the soon-to-be-established kingdom (Mark 9:30–37). On another occasion when Jesus talked about His fate, James and John responded by jockeying for positions of prestige and power (Mark 10:32–45). It was as if they had blocked out the possibility of His death while they dreamed about big offices in the new administration. Consequently, the significance of Mary's act was lost on the disciples, but it wasn't lost on Jesus. Jesus commended Mary for her sensitivity and defended her against her critics.

Words of Praise

When Martha went to Jesus with her complaint about Mary's lack of helpfulness, she asked Jesus to tell Mary to help her (Luke 10:40). But Jesus didn't do that. He continued to let Mary sit at His feet and learn from Him. About her, Jesus said, "Mary has chosen the good portion, which shall not be taken away from her" (Luke 10:42 RSV). Mary was pleasing Jesus more by listening to His teaching than she would have by rushing about with serving chores. Jesus gave her special consideration, including her, a woman, into His learning circle, and He said she had chosen "the good portion."

Jesus defended Mary against Judas and the other men when they complained of the waste of the expensive perfume. He reminded them that they would always have the poor with them, but they wouldn't always have Him. In other words, there are moments in life which do not come a second time. And if they are not acted on at once, they may never return. Mary was sensitive enough to realize this.

Mary had also seen far deeper than had the others. Her act was a pre-mortem memorial, an embalming before death. Preparing a body for burial involved washing it, applying spices, and wrapping it in strips of linen. As a presage, Mary applied to Him the very finest and most costly ointment. As we would say, she brought the flowers while He still could smell them.

In sitting at Jesus' feet, quietly listening and taking in His words, and in anointing His body with a lavish gift of perfume and love, Mary was caring for Jesus as a person, and that must have meant a great deal to Him. Jesus, who had helped so many, might have wanted to know that someone loved him for who He was, not just what He could do. Throngs had come to Him for help and gone away rejoicing! Yet few thought about Jesus' needs. Much of Jesus' life is illustrated in the healing of ten lepers. Only one of the ten thanked Him (Luke 17:12–19). Mary, though, thought about her benefactor. She expressed clearly that she saw, understood, and cared deeply. Her act of devotion must have given Him comfort as he faced the hard road that lay ahead.

About her extravagant gift, Jesus said, "Wheresoever the gospel shall be preached throughout the whole world, this also that she hath done shall be spoken of for a memorial of her" (Mark 14:9 KJV). When believers down the line—believers like us—look back at Mary's act, they will think, *Oh, how wonderful to have had the chance to minister to Jesus in such a special way.* We do have the chance if we don't let our sensitivity get blocked by busyness, selfishness, distractions, worries, or ambition.

We can sit at His feet and listen—really listen—to what Jesus has to say. We can show the devotion Mary exhibited and from time to time express our love in an extravagant way. When we are sensitive to what He wants and *respond accordingly,* we please Him just as Mary did.

chapter eight

The Women at the Cross:
A Christ Follower Is Loyal

Matthew 27:55–56
Mark 15:40–41
Luke 8:1–3
Luke 23:49
Luke 23:55–24:10
John 19:25–27

What quality do you value most in friends? Humor. Intelligence. Emotional honesty. Encouragement. Comfort. Trustworthiness. Understanding. Acceptance. Being good-natured. Common interests. Kindness. Affection. Consideration.

One quality I value highly is loyalty. I don't want fair weather friends. I want friends who will be there for me when I am successful and when I fail. I want friends who will stick with me through the thick and thin of life.

What quality do you value most when you're in a leadership position? I still would have to go with loyalty. Whether it is teaching Sunday school (Remember my outburst that I described in the Martha chapter?), directing a retreat, or planning a missions project, I need helpers I can rely on. Oh, I understand when committee members have to resign or when interest wanes. These things happen, but I thrive better and can serve more effectively when I am secure in knowing I can count on people. Over the long haul, I need and want faithful followers when I am leading.

Perhaps that's why I have such high admiration for the Galilean women who we featured in chapter 4. Their following of Christ wasn't just a whim or a spurt; they were faithful over the long haul, enduring all the way to the cross and beyond.

From Galilee to Jerusalem

The Galilean women traveled with Jesus and His twelve disciples, supported them out of their resources (Luke 8:1–3), and cared for their needs. They left their comfortable lifestyles to "rough it" on the road—cooking over open fires, camping out under the stars, and being in a different place every night.

They witnessed much as they journeyed with Jesus. At first, when they were traveling around Galilee with Him, Jesus experienced high public favor, but opposition developed against Him. The Jewish religious leaders were upset with Him because of who He associated with, because He taught with authority, and because He didn't practice many of their established observances and traditions. Consequently, the atmosphere around Jesus was often hostile and tense. The women saw the throngs deride Jesus; they heard His teaching challenged. His keenest opposition was in Jerusalem, in Judea, so it was risky for Jesus to leave Galilee to go there for the Passover. But He went anyway, and the Galilean women followed (Mark 15:41).

The Bible says many were in the group and names some of them:

• Mary Magdalene, Joanna, and Susanna (Luke 8:2–3), whom we already talked about in chapter 4.

• Mary, the mother of James the Less (one of the disciples) and Joses (Mark 15:40),

• Mary, the wife of Clopas (John 19:25),

• Salome, the wife of Zebedee and the mother of the two apostles James and John (Mark 15:40, Matthew 27:55–56).

• Mary, Jesus' mother (John 19:25), and

• His mother's sister (John 19:25), who could have been Clopas' wife or Salome.

Once in Jerusalem, it was hard to stay near Jesus. The city was so crowded, and many people wanted to be near Him. Still the women thought it important to be in the city. They could empathize with Jesus as they felt some of the intensity of the pressures that wrapped around Him. They heard people speculate about Jesus' future. They heard the religious leaders challenge and ridicule Him.

On Thursday night, Jesus spent the evening with the disciples. They ate the Passover meal together in an air of solemnity, as if death were hovering near. Talk of betrayal surfaced, and Peter said to Jesus, "I will never leave you" (Mark 14:29).

"Jesus said to Peter, 'I tell you that before the rooster crows two times tonight, you will say three times that you do not know me.' Peter answered even more strongly, 'I will never say that, even if I have to die with you!' And all the other disciples said the same thing" (Mark 14:30–31). And yet a short time later, when the Sanhedrin's police force arrested Jesus, "all the disciples left him and ran away" (Mark 14:50 TEV).

The next day, when Jesus was nailed to a cross, they weren't there either, except for John. But the Galilean women were present. They didn't deny Jesus, desert Him, or run away. They stood by Him during His darkest hour.

Close but Not Close

The women were close in spirit to Jesus as He suffered on the cross, but they stood "at a distance" watching the scene before them (Luke 23:49); they looked at their beloved Jesus on the cross from afar (Mark 15:40).

Perhaps the Roman soldiers, who were in charge of the execution, forbade them from getting any closer. They might have determined a point or a line beyond which spectators could not go.

Or the women might have stood back because of the malicious crowd, the rough soldiers, and the rowdy hecklers. The New King James Version says, "There were *also* women looking on from afar" (Mark 15:40, emphasis mine), as if women usually were not present. It was not a place women frequented, but these courageous, independent women wouldn't be deterred.

In Jerusalem, the women risked danger to be identified

with Jesus because He was regarded as a criminal. Who knew when the hostile crowds would start heckling them, or when the Sanhedrin, the Jewish court, would falsely accuse the women as they had Jesus?

Another reason they might have kept their distance from the cross was because of the horror of the scene. Even though they were courageous women, they would have been repulsed by the crucifixion, one of the cruelest forms of punishment ever invented by man. It was heart wrenching to watch the One they loved being tormented, reviled, humiliated, and in pain—so why were they there?

The Bible says the women were there to minister to Jesus (Matthew 27:55), but what kind of ministry was possible? There really wasn't anything they could do, was there?

The Ministry of Being There

The Galilean women had no power to free Jesus, no way to save Him, no way to undo what had been done. The members of the Sanhedrin, the Jewish court, had been determined to bring about Jesus' death. They were so determined that they lost all sense of good judgment, even ignoring their own rules of justice to have Jesus condemned. Even if the Sanhedrin retried Jesus, the women would not be allowed to testify on Jesus' behalf, because they did not regard the women as credible witnesses.

After reaching a guilty verdict, the Sanhedrin quickly got the Roman authorities to agree to put Jesus to death. Roman soldiers stood by to see that no one interfered and the execution was completed. The Galilean women had no influence with the mighty Roman Empire to get their procurator, Pontius Pilate, to reverse his decision.

From an outsider's perspective, it looked as if there was nothing the women could do, but the women didn't see it that way. They knew their presence would minister to Jesus. They knew the importance of "being there" for another, of having someone who cares about you to share emotionally and spiritually what you are experiencing.

The importance of this ministry dawned on me years ago when a friend lost her job. Afterward, Barbara tried to get unemployment compensation. Her request was denied. Barbara appealed and was granted a hearing.

She said to me, "Brenda, I'm scared. I've heard that employees don't have a chance, that the results always favor the employer. Yet I believe I have been treated unfairly."

"Would you like for me to go with you to the hearing?"

"Oh, would you please?"

The hearing was intense as Barbara was bombarded with questions. I sat where she could see me, so that any time she looked my way she would knowing someone was rooting for her. Even though Barbara lost her case, she profusely thanked me. Over and over, she said, "You'll never know what your being there meant to me."

In a few weeks I found out. In the middle of the night, I had to call an ambulance because my husband was experiencing extreme abdominal pain. As the paramedics took him to a hospital 25 miles away, I called a friend. I said, "I'm sorry to wake you," and then I explained what happened. I added, "I don't know why I called, Carileen. I guess I just needed someone to know."

Carileen said, "Do you want me to come to the hospital?"

"No, that won't be necessary. I'll be all right. Just pray for me."

When I arrived at the hospital thirty minutes later, *Carileen was there.* "You shouldn't have come," I said, but I was glad she had. What a long, lonely night it would have been as I waited for a diagnosis that didn't come until morning. I realized I needed more than her prayers; I needed her presence.

Those experiences helped me identify the ministry of "being there," to recognize it and appreciate it when I am the recipient and to try to give it when the opportunity presents itself. This is also why I believe the presence of the Galilean women was a valuable ministry to Jesus. In a matter of hours, He was arrested, deserted by His apostles, tried unfairly, ridiculed and spat upon, nailed to a cross, and taunted. He couldn't see the faces of Peter, Matthew, James, and others of His disciples. For a time, He would even feel forsaken by God. What a comfort it must have been to be able to look down from the cross and see the faithful women. Their loyalty must have been a solace to Him.

Not only did they want to comfort Him with their presence, they wanted to be there in case there was anything they could do. "They had followed Jesus from Galilee to care for his needs" (Matthew 27:55 NIV), so they stood, they watched, and they waited. If any kind of opportunity to help presented itself, they would be there, and just such an opportunity did occur.

What They Noticed

The curious came and went, but the women maintained their presence at the cross. Even when the awful darkness covered the earth, they did not leave.

As they huddled together, the women wondered what was going to happen to Jesus' body. If normal procedure were followed, the bodies of Jesus and the two thieves crucified alongside Him would be thrown into the nearest pit where they could be easily covered. Or more than likely, the bodies would be thrown like the carcasses of animals onto a burning garbage heap.

Fortunately, Joseph, a rich, pious Jew from Arimathea, who was a follower of Jesus and a member of the Sanhedrin, saved the body of Jesus from those awful alternatives (Mark 16:42–46, Matthew 27:57–60, Luke 23:50–54, John 19:38). Nicodemus, a Pharisee who once had a conversation with Jesus about being born again, helped him (John 19:39–42). The two of them partially prepared Jesus' body for burial, wrapped it in strips of linen, and quickly placed it in a new tomb provided by Joseph (John 19:38–42). But they weren't able to finish the burial preparations because time was running out. The Sabbath, which began at sundown on Friday, was quickly approaching, when all work must cease. Work included preparing a body for burial.

The Galilean women followed Joseph to the tomb, taking note of its location, its stone door, and how Jesus' body was laid in the tomb. They also noticed the unfinished ministrations. Their response was, "This must not be."

On their way back to the places they were staying, they acquired the materials for properly anointing Jesus' body.

They kept these materials ready for them to use after the Sabbath ended.

Very early on Sunday morning, they set out on their task. They went even though they had no idea how they would open the tomb. William Barclay describes, in *The Daily Study Bible*, "Tombs had no doors. When the word door is mentioned it really means opening. In front of the opening there ran a groove, and in the groove a circular stone as big as a cart-wheel." The women knew that it was beyond their strength to move a stone like that, but *they went anyway*.

Over and over I've witnessed ministering women replay this scene, and I never cease to be moved by their determination. Oh, the circumstances are different. It isn't a crucifixion, but it may be a harsh accident, a miscarriage, a death, a house fire, a flood, or some other tragedy. The women quickly connect with each other and go to help. As they go, carrying their casseroles, hams, and pies, they know they don't have words to say that will ease the suffering. They know they won't be able to explain what happened, and they can't change the situation, although they wish with all their hearts they could. They can't roll away the stone of heartache, *but they go anyway* to minister in the same kind of way the women at the cross did: to be present and to see if there's anything they can do. They hurt along with the hurting and with eyes always open to further ministry possibilities.

As simple as the ministries of "being there" and "seeing what can be done" are, not everyone responds this way. To minister like this is not easy. It is emotionally wrenching, time-consuming, physically draining, and often you feel totally inadequate. The Galilean women were bewildered, heartbroken, drenched in sorrow—but they endured. The overwhelming might of evil had no effect on their continuing loyalty. When Jesus died, the women did not rush to return immediately to Galilee. They didn't say, "Well, girls, let's go home. We've done all we can do here." They waited to see what would be done with the body of Jesus and found a way to continue to minister to Him. Why? Why were they so persistent in their devotion?

Loyalty Clings

People often come to Jesus for what He can do for them. They are in trouble and need a solution. They are sick and want to be healed. They are scared and want protection.

There's nothing wrong with coming to Jesus for these reasons, but we should not forget Him afterward. For many Galilean women, their being healed by Jesus cemented their relationship with Him. He had healed them of evil spirits and diseases. They were so grateful that they kept on ministering to Him. (The imperfect tense that Luke used to describe the ministering of the Galilean women in Luke 8:3 means "kept on ministering.") They loved Him because He first loved them. It was a love that would motivate them to be loyal. It was a love that sent them to the cross and kept them there even when their hearts were breaking. When the women went as early as possible on Sunday morning to the tomb, they went to anoint the dead body of One whom they loved.

Some have said that the women were loyal to the end because, unlike the men, they had nothing to fear, as

William Barclay says, "for so low was the public position of women that no one would take any notice of women disciples. There is more to it than that. They were there because they loved Jesus, and for them…perfect love had cast out all fear."

No adjectives are used in the Bible to describe the women at the cross, but if I were to describe them, I would use words such as courageous, devoted, loving, and most of all loyal, for they were continually faithful. The women served Jesus as He healed and preached. They gave of their substance to His work. They lamented His suffering. They watched as He patiently endured ridicule, ingratitude for His benefits (even some of His healings), and reproofs of His teachings. They were continually faithful to minister to Jesus because they loved Him. They weren't interested in what they could get, but rather in what they could give. They weren't seeking a reward, but they were rewarded.

Loyalty's Reward

The Galilean women were rewarded by being the first to know of Jesus' resurrection, but they didn't know this when they left that Sunday morning with their spices in hand. As they walked toward the sepulcher, they talked among themselves about how they might get the tomb opened (Mark 16:3). Imagine their surprise when they saw that the great stone had been rolled away (Mark 16:4). They entered the tomb and found Jesus' body was not there. Instead an angel was. He gave them an urgent message—a message for them and the disciples. Jesus would meet them in Galilee (Matthew 28:5–8; Mark 16:5–7).

A little later, some of the women saw two men in dazzling clothes appear to them at the tomb, and received words of comfort and instruction (Luke 24:4). Best of all were the words, "He is not here, but is risen!" (Luke 24:6 NKJV).

This was news to share! They hurried to tell the disciples and other believers (Luke 24:9). It was also news that drew them back to the tomb. Some of the women and Mary Magdalene returned to the tomb, but Mary ran on ahead. She was alone when she saw the resurrected Jesus (John 20:11–18). Then Jesus appeared to the other women (Matthew 28:9–10). They fell down at his feet, embraced them, and worshiped Him (Matthew 28:9).

Although a reward is not to be our motive for faithfully following Jesus, we will be rewarded. In a relationship where loyalty is present and active, the leader will draw closer and closer to his loyal followers and they to him. Then he will be able to open his heart to them, and to teach them things the unfaithful or the spasmodic follower can never learn. When we faithfully follow Jesus, ministering to Him and to others in His name, we will draw closer to Him. He will reveal Himself to us and teach us things the unfaithful will never learn. We can know the fellowship of His sufferings and experience the power of the resurrection (Philippians 3:10). We'll feel bubbling up inside us the same excitement the women felt when they realized Jesus was alive. *Ah, yes, He is here; He is alive!*

In contrast to the Galilean women's ministry when He was here in the flesh, our ministry to Him is to worship and to serve Him, to give Him our steadfast allegiance and devotion. It doesn't mean we will be perfect, or that the earnestness of our efforts won't vary at times, but it does mean that we will continue to have Jesus as the baseline of our lives. We will always be working to bring our will in line with His will. That's what being a Christ follower is all about. It's about being loyal to Him.

chapter nine

Dorcas:
A Christ Follower Does Good Things

Acts 9:36–43

I found Dorcas, also known as Tabitha, whose brief story is told in Acts 9:36–42, a little harder to get to know than some other New Testament women. She didn't receive as much attention from Bible commentators as other women like Mary Magdalene or Mary and Martha of Bethany did. The reason may be because her story is overshadowed by another story.

The Bigger Story

The Book of Acts is the story of the church—how it developed in Jerusalem, in Judea, and Samaria, and throughout the Roman Empire. In Jerusalem, after the Holy Spirit came, believers fellowshipped, learned, and worshiped together. As they grew numerically, the Jews began to see them as a threat to their faith. Persecution resulted, and consequently most of the believers fled, fanning out into the provinces of Judea and Samaria (Acts 8:1). Some ended up at Lydda and some at Joppa, where they witnessed to those living there, and congregations of believers were formed.

The apostles didn't flee Jerusalem when the other believers did, but from time to time they left to visit the new congregations. Peter, for example, went to Lydda: "There he met a man named Aeneas, who was paralyzed and had not been able to get out of bed for eight years. 'Aeneas,' Peter said to him, 'Jesus Christ makes you well. Get up and make your bed.' At once Aeneas got up" (Acts 9:33–34).

What a colossal event! Word spread. Folks in Joppa, a seacoast town about ten to fifteen miles northwest of Lydda, heard about it, and the timing couldn't have been better. Dorcas, one of their group, suddenly got sick and died. The Joppa believers sent two men to Peter with this message: "Come help us, and hurry."

With haste, Peter went to Joppa and found Dorcas laid out in the upstairs room with mourners crowded around. Putting the mourners out of the room, Peter knelt down and prayed. Then he said, "Tabitha, get up!"

She opened her eyes, and when she saw Peter, she sat up. He helped her up, and then he presented her alive to the believers!

In telling these two incidents, Luke, the author of Acts, wanted readers to see how miracles helped the gospel to spread and the church to grow.

After the healing of Aeneas, Luke wrote, "All the people living in Lydda and Sharon saw him, and they turned to the Lord" (Acts 9:35).

After the resurrection of Dorcas, he said, "The news about this spread all over Joppa, and many people believed in the Lord" (Acts 9:42).

So if you read Acts as a narrative, you can understand why Dorcas, the individual woman, may get overlooked. Who she is is incidental to the unfolding story. Her story could have been anyone's story—anyone whose story involved a miracle. Dorcas's story, though, is not incidental to our study because she was truly a Christ follower.

Her Distinction

Luke called Dorcas a "disciple." This is the first and only time in the New Testament this title is used to describe a woman.

In other chapters, I've described women as disciples of Jesus because in a general sense all earnest believers are. The word *disciple* means learner, pupil, or follower. In the New Testament, though, the word was also used as a label for followers of Jesus—male followers who surrounded Him or who were sent out by Him. Sometimes it was used to describe a large circle of followers. Sometimes it was used of a small circle such as the twelve apostles who were also called disciples. Dorcas is the only woman to be directly referenced as a disciple. Does this say something about Luke, the author? About the Christian community Dorcas was a part of? Or about the woman herself?

Luke was the New Testament writer who particularly took note of women. His Gospel is sometimes called the Gospel of Women, because he mentions them more than the other Gospel writers do. He recognized their presence in the life of Jesus and the contributions they made to His ministry.

Likewise, he gave attention to women as he wrote about the development of the church. In Acts, he used the term *disciple* to denote members of the Christian religion. When he learned about Dorcas as he researched the story, he discovered that she "was full of good works and charitable deeds" (Acts 9:36 NKJV), or as the New American Standard Bible says, "abounding with deeds of kindness and charity." It is not unusual for people to do good deeds—an occasional deed here and there—but to have a life abounding in good works could only come from someone who, in Luke's eyes, was a disciple of Jesus.

On the other hand, maybe Luke called her a disciple because the Joppa believers might have. In the interest of accurate reporting, he simply repeated what they said. You can tell they loved Dorcas by their urgency to get help. The delegation sent to Peter said to him, "Come at once."

Perhaps they had been recipients of some of her charity, or perhaps they deeply admired her for the good works she did. They saw her as doing Christ's work, and to them that made her a disciple. They didn't get into labels like "men's work" and "women's work." Titles and what's female and what's male may not have mattered as much here as it did in other places. Joppa was a seaport town where they were used to being accepting and tolerant as they interacted with different kinds of travelers. Their acceptance even included Simon, a tanner of leather (Acts 9:43). Jews didn't usually associate with tanners because their work, making animal hides into leather, involved contact with dead animals, making it an "unclean" job.

Perhaps Joppa's distance away from Jerusalem, the center of Jewish orthodoxy where rules were scrupulously kept, had something to do with their tolerance. Away from rule-conscious people and imbued with grace after believing in Jesus, they accepted Simon and Dorcas as disciples.

Whether the disciple label can be attributed to Luke or to the community, it would never have been used of Dorcas if she wasn't worthy to receive it. Who was she? What did she do? What was she like? We'll take the few details we have about her and see what we can learn, starting with her name.

What's in a Name

Dorcas's names tell us that she lived in two worlds—a Greek world and a Jewish world. Dorcas was her Greek name, and Tabitha, which is Aramaic, was the name used in her Jewish world. Joppa was in Judea, a Jewish province, and most of the Jews spoke Aramaic among themselves. It was their language of relationships and worship. This was especially true in Jerusalem, the center of Jewish orthodoxy. But Joppa was thirty-five miles northwest of Jerusalem and situated on the Mediterranean coast. Travelers came and went, travelers who spoke Greek, the dominant language of the Roman Empire.

On the street, in the marketplace, and doing business, Dorcas would have spoken Greek. At home and among friends, in her more intimate relationships, she spoke Aramaic.

Her names not only tell us about her environment, they might also tell us about her nature. Both Dorcas and Tabitha mean gazelle.

The gazelle is a small, graceful, and swift antelope. If Dorcas was truly like a gazelle, she was a small dynamo. Wouldn't she have had to have been to get as much done as she did? "She spent all her time doing good and helping the poor" (Acts 9:36). In particular, she made clothes. Making clothes in that day and time would have been time-consuming. There were no sewing machines; a garment had to be cut and sewn by hand. Where did she get her material? Did she buy it or did she have to weave it first? And spin the threads or yarns? That would have taken even longer.

Dorcas may have had special eyes, too. A gazelle is noted for its eyes—soft, brilliant, radiant, and glowing. Dorcas's eyes glowed with concern and compassion as she noticed the needy around her and used her skills to help them. Not everyone sees needs, but she did.

Eyes to See

Living by the sea, Dorcas saw numerous husbands and fathers depart and not return. The waters were perilous, and the dangers were many. Many men never returned, and they left behind bereaved and often destitute widows. Dorcas reached out to them, becoming their friend and benefactor.

No wonder the widows were so distraught when Dorcas died. They stood by Peter weeping and "showing the tunics and garments which Dorcas had made while she was with them" (Acts 9:39 NKJV).

I chuckled at the words of one Bible commentator who said, "notice the uniquely female detail to this story." He was referring to the widows pointing out the garments Dorcas had made as if she had made the clothes for them. And she may have. The Bible doesn't say which it was—clothes for the widows or clothes for the needy—but suppose she had made clothes for the widows? What would have been the wisdom of that? It could have been that she wanted them to be protected and warm against the elements, but Dorcas also may have known, as many women suffering loss know, that some days it may be the outer garment that holds the inner woman together.

You lie in bed in the early hours of the morning, huddled in the darkness, wondering if you can face the day. You don't want to smile and greet your coworkers. You don't want to answer the inevitable question, "How are you?" that comes with a direct look that says, "How are you *really?*" This wasn't the future you had envisioned for yourself; you just want to crawl back into your past, but there's a job to keep and bills to pay. So finally you drag yourself out of bed, wash your face, comb your hair, shed your pajamas, and put on a suit. You smile to yourself as you button the jacket and look in the mirror. *I know why they call this a power suit now. I feel better. I just might make it through another day.*

The right clothes can make you feel more confident, whether it's facing the day, giving a speech, applying for a job, or trying to meet a goal. I had a Dorcas in my life when I was a struggling seminary student. I wasn't a widow, but I was single and broke. I didn't complain about what I didn't have to wear, but my pastor's wife noticed. She didn't sew but she knew a woman in our church who did. Alba went to her and said, "Brenda needs some clothes. Can you help?" This woman was a whiz with a needle, with finding bargain materials, and with creating something new out of something old. She took some of her clothes and reworked them for me, plus made me some new things, and having this new wardrobe lifted my spirits and increased my confidence as a student.

To talk about how the right clothes help a woman is not to contradict Jesus' admonition to "Take no thought for tomorrow...what you shall put on" (Matthew 6:25). In that passage, Jesus is warning about worrying excessively or becoming too consumed by clothes. But the other side is that clothes can make a difference in attitude, in confidence, and in protection, so providing clothes for others can be a ministry.

Regardless of whether Dorcas made clothes exclusively for the widows or whether she made them for needy people in general, she still offered the widows something they needed—a group.

Doing Life Together

When Peter presented Dorcas alive, he called the saints *and the widows* (Acts 9:40–41). Christians are called *saints* in the New Testament, a word that means "different." Christians are different from others. Their difference lies in the fact that they are chosen for the special purposes of God. To refer to "widows" as a separate group does not mean that the widows could not be or were not saints. It just means that a distinct group had formed—"The Widows." This group could have included Christians and non-Christians. What drew them together were their losses, and Dorcas was their leader.

As Dorcas sewed, she probably invited the widows to join her. She knew what someday research would verify—that sewing is therapeutic. Studies have shown that sewing helps decrease heart rate and blood pressure for people skilled at sewing and for those just learning how.

Dorcas also knew the women would benefit from being with others. Whether they were skilled or not, they could cut out patterns, thread needles, or sweep up scraps. Some could prepare snacks for those who sewed. And as they did, chatter occurred—conversation that included tears, confession of fears and worries, problem solving, and sometimes laughter. Isn't it amazing how there's usually one woman who can put a humorous spin on life's worries so laughter erupts and relieves? And after being a part of a group like this, you notice your shoulders feel lighter and you feel a little more hopeful about your future. Now, none of these women would ever say, "I'm going over to Dorcas's to be renewed in my spirit or get help with a personal problem." No, but she could say, "I'm going to Dorcas's to sew for the needy," and in the process receive spiritual nourishment, practical help, and emotional support.

Dorcas was a woman who saw the need for companionship, understood it, and who drew women together, giving them courage and hope. Those eyes that glowed with compassion were the eyes of an understanding woman. Were they the eyes of one who had been hurt or known loss?

Empathetic Eyes

Some read Dorcas's story as if she were a widow, almost as if she had to be. Otherwise, how would she have known about the plight of widows? Why would she have been motivated to help? A widow would know and understand the pain of other widows. If she were, her experience would have given her empathy and understanding for other widows. But would she have had to have been a widow herself to minister to widows?

Some would say yes. *You can only understand my needs if you are in the same boat or have been where I am.* But truly compassionate eyes can have an appreciation for another person's pain—and act to relieve it—even if they haven't experienced it themselves. Jesus did.

Jesus healed the lame and sick because He hurt for

them (Matthew 14:14).

Moved by gentle compassion, He touched the untouchables, the outcasts who were scorned by society (Mark 1:40–42).

Jesus' heart stirred in tender response to lost souls and those with fumbling faith (Matthew 9:36).

Jesus multiplied the loaves and fish because people were hungry (Matthew 14:13–21).

Jesus was sensitive to the widow of Nain who lost her only son (Luke 7:11–15). Jesus saw her pain and brought her son back to life. She didn't even have to ask.

Jesus empathized with the woman caught in adultery. He understood how humiliated, angry, and frightened she must have been, and he defended her against the angry crowd (John 8:1–11).

Whether Dorcas had the eyes of a gazelle or not, we don't know for sure. We do know she had the eyes of Jesus—compassionate eyes. And like Jesus, she not only saw, she acted.

Faith Alive

Dorcas "was full of good works and charitable deeds *which she did*" (Acts 9:36 NKJV, emphasis mine). How significant are the last three words! Too many well-meaning people see needs and do nothing. They sit around and talk about charitable works that should be done and don't lift a finger. This is what James was warning us about in his little epistle.

"My brothers, what good is it for someone to say that he has faith if his actions do not prove it?...Suppose there are brothers or sisters who need clothes and don't have enough to eat. What good is there in your saying to them, 'God bless you! Keep warm and eat well!'—if you don't give them the necessities of life? So it is with faith: if it is alone and includes no actions, then it is dead."
—James 2:14–17

Dorcas not only saw needs and thought of ways to relieve needs, but she also carried out her plans, patterning her life after Jesus'. No wonder she was called a disciple! In who she was and what she did, she reflected Jesus. She had learned from Him, and in the process took on His nature—a nature that pleases God (James 1:27).

And I wouldn't have realized this about Dorcas if I hadn't taken the time to look at the details of her resurrection story, and I'm so glad I did. Her story may be overshadowed by a bigger one, but she herself casts a long shadow. Many women—and men—throughout history have sought to emulate the life of Dorcas by establishing "Dorcas Societies" that hold humanitarian ideals, engage in various relief activities, and seek to do good. Just type "Dorcas Societies" in your Internet search engine and you'll see what I mean.

Her shadow reached through history and touched me, too, reminding me of a truth that's easy to forget: "God has made us what we are, and in our union with Christ

Jesus he has created us for a life of good deeds" (Ephesians 2:10). How I do that may be different than the way Dorcas did it. No one would want to wear a garment that I sewed! But the important thing is that I do what I can. Like Dorcas, we all fit into a bigger story—God's story. If I want to be His disciple, then I have to ask, "What's my part? What can I do?"

chapter ten

Lydia:
A Christ Follower Opens
Her Heart and Home

Acts 16:11–15, 40

Jesus used parables to teach many things, one of which was that some people will be more receptive to our messages than others. He compared it to finding the right kind of soil in which to sow seeds (Mark 4:3–8). When seeds fall in good soil, plants sprout, grow, and bear grain (4:8). When Paul planted seeds in Philippi, he found rich soil in the heart of a woman named Lydia.

Paul was a trained rabbi who became a Christ follower. He was so passionate about Christ that he traveled throughout the Roman Empire telling others about the Christ, Jews first and then Gentiles. He was in Troas, on the coast of Asia Minor, when he had a vision of "a man of Macedonia" begging him, "Come over into Macedonia, and help us" (Acts 16:9 KJV). Almost immediately, Paul and his traveling companions, Silas, Luke, and Timothy, "left by ship from Troas and sailed straight across to Samothrace, and the next day to Neapolis" (Acts 16:11). This was a significant crossing because Paul was now in Europe, ready to launch a ministry on a new continent.

Paul could have stopped at Neapolis and officially have been in Macedonia, but Paul was a strategist. When Paul chose places to preach and establish the gospel, he chose places that were influential and important to a whole area. Philippi, a leading city of the district of Macedonia, was that kind of place.

While not a really large city, Philippi was a prosperous commercial center, located on an important Roman road that connected Europe and Asia. A strong Roman colony was established in this rich city.

Roman colonies were the focal points of the great Roman road systems. They were founded to keep the peace, to ensure the loyalty of the population, and to command the critical centers of Rome's vast empire. To start a church in Philippi would be a great triumph.

So from Neapolis, Paul and his companions went inland to Philippi, to establish their hub for reaching Macedonia for Christ. In contrast, Lydia was in Philippi for a totally different reason.

On Business

Lydia immigrated to Philippi from the region of Thyatira in the province of Asia. She "was a dealer in purple cloth" (Acts 16:14). Being a "dealer" could mean several things:

• She could have overseen the manufacture of purple cloth. After arriving in Philippi, Lydia could have set up an operation for making fabric, employing people to do the work because producing textiles was traditionally woman's work.

• She could have been a seller of cloth produced in Thyatira. As a company's representative, she might have been sent to Philippi because it was a prosperous community, and wealthy women were the primary purchasers of purple cloth.

• Instead of the cloth, Lydia may have sold dyes. The people of Thyatira were well known for their skill in the manufacture and use of purple dye, and perhaps Lydia represented a firm that sold dyes.

• Or she could have sold both cloth and dye.

Whatever form her business took, she would have needed employees to help her, so her position would have been one of influence and authority.

Her business might have also made her wealthy or, at least, given her a good income because both the cloth and dyes in hues ranging from red to purple were bought by royalty and by wealthy people.

She not only ran a business, Lydia owned her own home. She probably had some servants, and some family members may have lived with her. No mention is made of a husband. She may have been widowed; in that time and place, this was more likely than being divorced or never married.

Lydia was a Gentile businesswoman in Philippi to deal in purple. Paul was a Jewish Christian in town to sow seeds of the gospel. They traveled in two different circles with two different agendas. How did the two connect?

Strategy's First Step

If you were new in a town and you had an important message for the citizens, how would you get the word out? Go to the local newspaper and ask the publisher to do a feature on you? Ask to speak at the service clubs? Stand on a soapbox on a corner and shout your message through a megaphone?

To spread the gospel, Paul usually attended the local Jewish synagogue when he visited a new city. On the first Sabbath after his arrival, he attended synagogue services. There he would be assured of having a ready audience, for there was a time in the services for rabbis to speak. Unfortunately, few Jews lived in Philippi. There wasn't enough to constitute a synagogue. All it took was ten Jewish men. F. F. Bruce says in his commentary on Acts that "No number of women could compensate for the absence of even one man necessary to complete the quorum of ten." Since there was no synagogue, Paul looked for Jews who might be meeting somewhere else on the Sabbath.

Paul and his three companions "went out of the city to the riverside" (Acts 16:13). Paul knew that when

Jews were unable to have a synagogue they would gather in a place of prayer, usually by the riverside.

On the banks of the river, Paul and his associates found a group of women. They "sat down and talked to the women who gathered there" (Acts 16:13). As they conversed, the men learned that the women normally gathered there each Sabbath for prayer. In Philippi there were not ten Jewish men to make up a synagogue, but there were faithful women meeting to worship.

As he observed the women, Paul's mental wheels must have turned. *Here's just a small group of women and no men. Where am I going to gain listeners and responders to build a church? I need some influential men to establish a beachhead for the gospel in Philippi.*

For a moment, he might have even questioned the vision that led him to Philippi. *Where was the man in the vision?* And yet right in the middle of that group was Lydia, who would provide him with all the fertile soil he needed. He didn't realize it just yet; he would have to see for himself after "the Lord opened her heart to respond to Paul's message" (Acts 16:14 NIV).

A Receptive Heart

When Jesus told parables, He often punctuated them with these words: "He who has ears to hear, let him hear." As he used everyday circumstances and objects to describe spiritual truths, some people didn't pick up on the meaning. They just heard Him talk about circumstances and objects; but others, those with spiritual ears, grasped the meaning of the stories.

Lydia had that kind of spiritual sensitivity, a sensitivity that she had already been heeding. She had "ears to hear" because she was a worshiper of God (Acts 16:14), otherwise known by Jews as a "God-fearer."

"God-fearer" was a term used in New Testament times to describe a Gentile who accepted the truth of the Jewish religion but who did not become a full convert. Weary of the many gods permeating their culture and frustrated by ancestral faiths, some Gentiles were attracted by the simple monotheism of Jewish synagogue worship. Repulsed by the immorality around them, they turned to the pure ethics of Jewish religion.

God-fearers believed in God. They attended synagogue services, participated in prayers and Scripture lessons, and some even practiced Sabbath observances and abstained from eating forbidden foods.

If a Gentile God-fearer believed in God, why didn't he or she convert to Judaism? Many were repulsed by circumcision, which was required of all Jewish men. Others were turned off by the Jewish Law. Peter had once described the Law as a heavy load on the backs of Jews. An outsider hearing those rules might have thought they were just too much ("I could never keep them all") or too specific ("Not pull out a gray hair on the Sabbath? Ridiculous.") It may have been the Law that kept Lydia from becoming a Jew, because according to it she was "unclean."

Purple dyes were extracted either from the veins of shellfish or from the roots of the madder plant. If Lydia's dyes came from the shellfish, she would have been considered "unclean" by Jewish law, a sobering reminder to her of the severity of the Law.

Still, Lydia recognized a need in her life. This successful, independent, wealthy businesswoman and homeowner who seemed to have everything, didn't. She needed God and she needed a standard to live by. She may have recognized this and became a God-fearer before she ever left Thyatira, because there was a Jewish community in that city. Or she could have become a believer after arriving in Philippi, because the purity of Judaism would have been in stark contrast to the many pagan divinities and cults functioning in Philippi. Judaism provided her an oasis in the midst of the spiritual and moral drought that prevailed around her.

She worshiped God and she wanted to associate with others who did too, so she was present for prayer when Paul arrived at the riverside.

Lydia listened, always an indication of a receptive heart, and heard Paul's message of grace. What he spoke about was not a religion of rules and regulations, but it was about God's Son dying on the cross for her sins. Paul said that if she believed Jesus was sent from God, He would accept her just as she was, forgive her of her sins, and forever be her companion.

What good news! Lydia believed Paul, accepted his message, confessed her sins, acknowledged Jesus as Lord, and became *Paul's first convert in Europe*. She was immediately baptized and her whole household joined. It was just as if Lydia reached out her arms and gathered them into the household of faith.

Then her arms opened wider. She invited Paul and his associates to stay in her home. They didn't respond as readily to her invitation as those in her household did. In fact, the four missionaries were reluctant to accept, but Lydia "prevailed upon" them (Acts 16:15 NASB). Lydia not only opened her heart; she wanted to open her home as well.

Open Heart, Open Home

Many women like to be prepared for company. They don't extend invitations unless there's enough food in the refrigerator, the house is clean, and family members are forewarned.

And then there are other women—women whom I describe as being larger than life—who would respond as Lydia did and offer an invitation on the spot. They are women who can handle a lot and still be generous with others. Lydia could manage her business, her household, being in a strange land, and still take in strangers. Her open heart was a big heart.

Or it could have been that she simply cared. She had been new to town once and knew what that was like. She saw it this way: "These men are strangers in town. I know from experience that local inns are notoriously bad, and I have good accommodations. I'll offer them a place to stay." And so she did.

This concern may very well have been mixed with gratitude. She was genuinely happy and relieved to know that she was accepted by God by believing in His Son. She was grateful to Paul and his associates for coming to Philippi, and she wanted to show her appreciation.

Or the invitation might have been prompted by her enthusiasm over finding Christ. That might have been the reason for her saying to the missionaries, "Stay in my house *if* you have decided that I am a true believer in the Lord" (Acts 16:15, emphasis mine). In her exuberance, she wanted to know more. "Fellows, I am going to need more help. I want to know more about Jesus and how He wants me to live. I want to learn from you and glean from your experiences."

I remember pestering my mother to invite visiting evangelists, missionaries, and denominational workers to our home when I was a child. Even though the conversations were mostly among adults, I delighted in hearing them talk. I listened to their stories, learned from them, laughed frequently, and was inspired. They made me want to grow up and to be like them someday. I'm grown up now, and I still find it a joy to entertain God's workers in my home. Around the table, over coffee, I learn far more than when I am sitting in the pew and they are speaking from the platform. So I can understand why Lydia wanted the missionaries to stay, but what I can't figure out is their reluctance to accept her invitation. Why did she have to insist?

The Men's Reluctance

Maybe it wasn't good manners in their culture to readily accept an invitation. Sometimes in ours we have to converse back-and-forth a bit before we can say actually say yes.

"Why don't you stay with us?"

"Oh, no, we couldn't."

"Why not? We'd love to have you."

"That's awfully nice of you to offer, but we wouldn't want to put you out."

"Oh, it wouldn't be any trouble."

"But there are four of us."

"We'll manage. Nothing to it. We insist."

"All right, thank you!"

Or maybe the missionaries wanted to see if she were trustworthy. They didn't really know her and perhaps she was like the many female cult leaders in Philippi. She might be a little weird. (The other side of the coin is that Lydia didn't know these men either. She didn't know, for example, how Paul was often run out of the towns he visited. Her invitation was a fearless act on her part, showing how much God had moved in her life and how hungry she was to know more.)

Another reason why the men might have been reluctant to stay with her is that they felt uncomfortable around Lydia. As a capable, independent, decisive, assertive businesswoman and traveler, Lydia was not typical. She was not like the women the men were used to associating with. As mentioned in chapter 4, Roman society did not offer women very many business opportunities. Perhaps they just didn't know how to respond to such an unusual woman.

Fortunately, the men overcame their reluctance and accepted Lydia's invitation, and it was a good thing, because the seed planted in Lydia sprouted and grew into a well-established church.

The Church at Philippi

When Lydia provided the four missionaries with a place to stay, she provided them much more. She gave them a nucleus to begin a church. Bonnie Thurston, in her book *Women in the New Testament*, explains, "Because a number of people were required to produce and dye cloth, Lydia's household might have been extensive, and may thus have been a considerable community of Christians after its conversion."

She provided them with contacts. As a successful businesswoman, Lydia had a number of clients to whom she could have introduced Paul and the others. Plus her enthusiasm for the gospel would have made her eager to do so.

She gave them a base of operations. As Paul, Silas, Timothy, and Luke mingled in the marketplace, talking with people and witnessing to them, they could always say, "If you want to know more or if you have any questions, we'll be at Lydia's."

She gave them a place to meet. While the group continued—at least for a while—to gather at the place of prayer by the riverside (Acts 16:16), Lydia's house also became a meeting place (Acts 16:40), as homes often did in the first century. New Testament congregations were dependent upon homes for meeting places, starting with those early days in Jerusalem when they went from house to house breaking bread (Acts 2:46).

At Lydia's house, people could congregate because she was hospitable and warm. At her house, where the missionaries were staying, you could get your questions answered, you could experience God's spirit and

Christian fellowship, and you could learn and worship. It was a place where strangers were welcomed with love and where encouragement was shared.

That's why, when Paul and Silas got in trouble, they went to Lydia's.

Trouble in River City

Nowhere were people prouder of being Roman citizens than in the Roman colonies. Their pride was exemplified in their behavior. They spoke the Roman language, they wore Roman clothes, they observed Roman customs, their magistrates had Roman titles, and they observed Roman ceremonies. Their strong pride sometimes resulted in animosity toward Jews. (This may help explain why there were few Jews living in Philippi.)

You can hear the Roman pride pulsating through the charge against Paul and Silas when they are dragged before the Roman magistrates after setting a slave girl free from a spirit of divination. She made money for her owners by telling fortunes. Mercifully, Paul commanded the spirit to come out of the tormented girl.

"At that moment the spirit left her. When the owners of the slave girl realized that their hope of making money was gone, they seized Paul and Silas and dragged them before the magistrates" (Acts 16:18-19 NIV). They said, *"These men are Jews,* and are throwing our city into an uproar by advocating customs unlawful for *us Romans* to accept or practice."

Others heard and joined in the protest. They beat Paul and Silas, and the magistrates threw them in jail.

Miraculously, an earthquake threw open the prison doors, and freed the prisoners from their chains. When the jailer saw the open doors, he was about to kill himself when Paul called out to him. Paul never missed a chance to witness! He won the jailer and his household to the Lord (adding more people to the growing body of believers in Philippi!). Still Paul and Silas were going to have to leave town. They had worn out their welcome.

Paul must have said, "We had better tell the other believers what happened before we go. If they hear about our being beaten and jailed, they are going to be discouraged."

Silas replied, "You're right. Besides, we can't leave without saying goodbye."

Paul and Silas knew where they would find the believers. They would be at Lydia's, of course.

While Paul and Silas wanted to encourage the believers, I suspect that Paul and Silas were also encouraged by the goodbye visit to Lydia's. It was a reminder as they continued to journey deeper into Europe that even when they can't see fertile soil right away, it may very well be right there. Lydia was eager to learn the truth from the start, and then she generously and freely offered what she had to establish the church.

As the city fathers escorted Paul and Silas out of town, they went knowing the church at Philippi was off to a good start because Christ had transformed a Macedonian woman, who then opened her heart and home to the believers' church.

chapter eleven

Eunice and Lois:
Christ Followers Nurture Faith in Others

Acts 16:1–5
2 Timothy 1:5
2 Timothy 3:14–15

I'll never forget the morning my youngest son left for the Marines. I awoke experiencing conflicting feelings. I didn't want Ben to go, and I didn't want him to stay!

I did want him to experience adventure and see the world, and those were the reasons he joined the Marines. I wouldn't have wanted to stifle his dreams for anything, but I dreaded the separation. I would miss him, plus I was fearful about the dangers he would face and concerned about the temptations he would encounter. As I busied myself preparing breakfast, I knew that any moment the recruiter would arrive to whisk Ben away, and I would be left holding a heart full of mixed emotions.

When I studied Eunice's life, I wondered if she might have had similar feelings when her son Timothy was leaving to become one of Paul's coworkers. Paul met Timothy, Eunice, and her mother Lois when he came to Lystra on his first missionary journey. Now Paul was back, and he wanted to take Timothy, her only child, with him when he left.

Eunice was happy that Paul chose Timothy; he had seen what a fine young man he was. She was also pleased Timothy wanted to serve Christ by going with Paul. But she would miss him greatly. Theirs had been a special relationship, for she was not only her son's mother, she was his teacher.

Passing on the Faith

In one sense all mothers are teachers, but in the Greco-Roman world of the first century, eldest sons were expected to learn and pass on, and to defend, the traditions and the honor of their families. Timothy was not only Eunice's oldest child, he was her only child, so she poured her values into him.

At first, when he was a small child, Eunice passed on her Jewish faith to Timothy. She and her mother, Lois, taught him the Jewish law, stories, traditions, and customs. She wasn't free to teach as much as she wanted to because her husband was a Gentile. He did not share her faith, and he prevented Timothy from being circumcised, a covenant ceremony very important to Jews. While home education usually was the responsibility of the mother, circumcision was the responsibility of the father. As a Greek, her husband considered it mutilation to the body and wouldn't allow it. Thankfully, though, her husband didn't interfere with teaching in many other ways, so she and Lois gave Timothy's education earnest effort.

Their earnestness to nurture Timothy's faith became even stronger after they became Christians. Lois became a Christian first, then Eunice, and then Timothy. The expectation was that what they taught Timothy would continue to the next generation and the next. They also wanted their faith, whether through them or Timothy, to extend to their community, because few Jews or Christians lived in Lystra.

The two women did a good job teaching Timothy and nurturing his faith. Paul had good things to say about him, and the believers in Lystra and Iconium spoke well of Timothy. He was just the kind of person you liked to have around. No wonder Paul wanted him for a companion. Eunice did too! Her home would be an emptier place without him.

Thank goodness, her mother Lois was living with her. Lois could understand her mixed emotions over Timothy's leaving. The two women had shared much through the years, and it was only natural that Eunice turned to her now.

Mother-Daughter Talk

While they were mending Timothy's tunics, Eunice thought out loud, "If Paul hadn't come by Lystra on his first journey, I wouldn't have to say goodbye to Timothy now."

Lois said, "I know, I know, but of course, we wouldn't be Christians now either, and I wouldn't have wanted to miss knowing Jesus. Would you?"

"You're right. I'm glad I'm a Christian, but…"

"But what?"

"I didn't know that when I accepted Christ, it would mean giving up my child. I had assumed, in the way that most mothers do, he would stay nearby. For years, I had counted on his establishing a Jewish home—and after our conversion, a Christian home. In my mind's eye, I saw him passing on the Scriptures we taught him to his children. He would initiate the Jewish feasts in his home and pass on stories of Jesus."

Then Eunice gasped as a painful new thought occurred to her. "Grandchildren. Does Timothy's leaving mean I might not have grandchildren? Will Timothy get married? Or will he stay single like Paul? If he marries, where will he live? Who knows where Paul's travels will take Timothy? Does this mean I might never have grandchildren living nearby to hold in my arms and play with them?" Tears slipped down her cheeks as she said, "Must I give up the dream of grandchildren, too, in addition to giving up my son?"

For a moment, Lois said nothing. Eunice's grief was too fresh for a snappy, ready response. Yet she knew—for their sake, for Timothy's sake, and most of all for Christ's sake— she needed to bolster Eunice so she could let him go. She gently tried to change the course of the conversation.

"Grandparenting is precious, isn't it? I know I have

really enjoyed my relationship with Timothy. It was certainly a delight to help you teach him. I have a lot of wonderful memories of our time together. As soon as he could talk, we were teaching him the *Shema*. Do you remember how hard it was for us all to get through Leviticus?"

A smile crossed Eunice's face. "Yes, it was, wasn't it?" Shaking her head in disbelief, she went on, "I don't know why Jews insist on beginning a child's education with Leviticus. Maybe if we had had a synagogue here or lived nearer the Temple in Jerusalem, it might have been easier to teach Leviticus."

"If there had been a synagogue here, we wouldn't have the privilege of teaching Timothy as much as we did. We would have had to send him to synagogue school when he turned six."

"I'll always be glad we had the time with Timothy that we did."

"You're talking like we'll never see him again."

Eunice smiled again. "I didn't mean it quite like that, although as extensive as Paul's travels are and as dangerous as they are, we might not. Have you noticed how many close calls and skirmishes that Paul has told us about? And surely you remember his first trip to Lystra? People here stoned him. And after he had healed a man who had been crippled from birth! The people just couldn't see how beneficial Christ's power would be to their lives. Remember how, for a while, we thought Paul was dead? It was a scary time. Oh, Mother, what if Timothy ends up being rejected or even stoned?"

"It would break my heart, but we can't say it could

never happen. Remember Paul told us from the beginning that having troubles is part of the Christian life. Besides, Timothy has heard all of Paul's stories, and he is still willing to follow Paul."

"Isn't Timothy brave?" said Eunice proudly. "Why, he didn't even flinch when Paul told him he would have to be circumcised. The surgery would have been a lot less painful if it had been done when Timothy was a baby, as I wanted."

"Actually, I find it hard to understand why Paul is insisting that Timothy have it done since we are made right with God by grace, not by a symbolic ceremony."

"Oh, Paul is just so conscientious. He wants to reach the Jews in our region. They think it is important, and most of them know Timothy's father was a Greek and therefore assume Timothy wasn't circumcised. Paul is meticulous about keeping the faith; he has such high standards." As she said that, Eunice's face brightened. "Just think. This man of high standards chose Timothy to go with him. That speaks well of Timothy, doesn't it?"

"It speaks well of you, too. You raised him well, nurturing a strong faith in him and grounding him in Scripture."

"I couldn't have done it without you."

"I am just glad we had the privilege, and now we have the privilege of passing his training over to someone else. We've prepared the way, and now it is time for Paul to pick up where we left off and add to Timothy's training and development."

Strengthened by her conversation with her mother, Eunice realized she needed to let Timothy go. Timothy was a Christ follower just as she was, and that meant encouraging him to go wherever Christ led him. He would help Paul strengthen the churches, help them grow, be a missionary to the Jews and to the Gentiles, and an evangelist like Paul. When Timothy entered the room to collect the tunics, she held out her arms for one last hug. She didn't cling, though. He wasn't a child any longer; he was a man called by God to serve Him. Besides, Paul was at the door, calling, "Timothy, are you ready?" And Eunice knew that he was; she had prepared him well.

With his mother and his grandmother's blessing, Timothy left with Paul. For years, Timothy was his faithful and diligent coworker. "And as they went through the cities….the churches were strengthened in the faith, and increased in number daily" (Acts 16:4–5, NKJV). Eventually Paul entrusted him with the responsibility of leading a church. Paul appreciated Timothy's "genuine faith" (2 Timothy 1:5 NKJV) and recognized the source of it, always reminding Timothy of his spiritual roots (2 Timothy 1:5, 3:14–15). His mother and his grandmother had taught him well.

Teaching Them to Observe

Eunice and Lois nurtured Timothy's faith, and their story can nurture ours, too. It reminds us that all Christ followers are to cultivate the faith of others. It is not enough just to introduce people to Christ; we must also teach, train, and educate them. After telling His disciples to "go" and "make disciples," He said to teach "them to observe all things that I have commanded you" (Matthew 28:20 NKJV).

This doesn't mean we must all teach in the same way.

Eunice and Lois show us how two women nurtured the faith of a child in the home. This would have involved direct teaching, formal and informal conversations, activities, interaction, and being a loving example.

Paul picked up where they left off, adding geography (traveling from place to place), hands-on experience, coaching on the job, and later letters, when Paul put Timothy in charge of the church at Ephesus. A strong mentor-protégé or father-son relationship developed between them. Paul called Timothy "my own son in the faith" (1 Timothy 1:2) and "my dearly beloved son" (2 Timothy 1:2).

For many women, nurturing faith in others means investing in their children and grandchildren as Eunice and Lois did. They may not do it in the same *way* as Eunice and Lois did, but their primary focus for developing faith in others is the children they are related to. They may do it through homeschooling, taking responsibility for all their children's education with the spiritual being one part of it. Or they may let others teach them math, English, and social studies and have Bible reading and memorization as family activities.

For other women, nurturing another's faith may involve a relationship with someone like Paul had with Timothy—someone who is not our relative but whom we can influence. It may be a child in a Sunday school class, the teenager who delivers the newspaper, or a young mother in the neighborhood who needs help with her children. Whether we have borne children, adopted them, or neither, we can all have "children in the faith."

Ways to Nurture

Some women nurture faith in others by teaching Bible studies or leading missions organizations. Others become involved in parachurch organizations where they disciple new believers.

Some prefer direct teaching, such as sharing a specific body of material, like teaching about the gifts of the Spirit or how to be a Christian mom. Other women teach indirectly by being an example or a role model. Eileen, the woman you met in chapter three who started the Haven of Rest for prisoner's families, learned her faith at the knee of her mother Nell, a passionate Christian and an enthusiastic supporter of missions.

"Missionaries blew her mind," remembers Eileen. Nell wanted deeply to become a missionary, but the Lord said, "Your responsibilities are to your family. Teach them about missions," a command which Nell followed faithfully. Most importantly, she modeled for her children a life of prayer, sacrificial giving, and faith in God's provision.

Eileen's family was poor, and she remembers a time her mother had no money to give to the missions offering. Nell prayed fervently, asking God to provide a way for her to give. As she prayed, God reminded her of an old penny she had saved, Eileen recalls. Nell took the coin to a collector, sold it, and gave the money to missions." (Her story is told in the April 2003 *Missions Mosaic* magazine).

With a faith background like that, no wonder Eileen could embark on a mission of raising thousands of dollars to build the Haven of Rest.

Cultivating faith in others can be a long-term commitment, such as in a mentoring, discipling, or parenting. It can also happen in a one-time encounter. You open your Bible on an airplane and teach the person in the seat next to you about the armor of God and how it helps a person stand firm in the faith. You are in the laundromat and you notice a young woman crying. You offer her a tissue, engage her in conversation, and before you know it, you are telling her the Bible story of Hagar crying in the wilderness. You reassure her that just as God saw Hagar, He sees her.

A woman doesn't have to be particularly articulate to promote and sustain faith in others. I think of my own mother in this regard. She was not a teacher or a public speaker, although she would try when our church desperately needed Sunday school teachers. One story that gets "told" and "retold" in our family is about how she tried to teach a group of girls in their early teens. She was doing her best, but the girls wouldn't be quiet. My youngest sister, who was in the group, took charge. Linda stopped the class and said firmly and authoritatively, "Shut up, girls," and they were so shocked they immediately quieted down. Then Linda looked at Mom and said, "Okay, go ahead. You can teach now."

My mother would never have received any formal teaching awards, but she receives accolades from her daughters for the faith example that she lived before us. Like Eunice, she worshiped alone, although my father professed to be a Christian. My mother had a faith that persevered through wars, sicknesses, financial hard times, and raising five children. I never realized more fully the impact of her faith on mine than I did September 11, 2001. As I waited for word from a son who lived and worked in Washington, D.C., I felt fragile and shaky as if I were going to fall apart. I also began to imagine what else might happen now that the door was opened to this kind of terrorism. As I paced the floor, I thought of my mother and how she had survived tough times, and I knew then that I would, too. Whatever came, I would face it because my mother, in who she was, nurtured my faith. When Paul needed to put some nerve in Timothy, he said, "Continue in what you have learned and have firmly believed, *knowing from whom you learned it*" (2 Timothy 3:14 RSV, emphasis mine). I knew from whom I had learned, and it made all the difference in my response.

The variety of ways to nurture faith in others is so endless that none of us should feel like we can't do it. Neither should we leave off doing it if the conditions aren't perfect. Just think how defeated Eunice might have felt if she had let her husband's lack of faith be an obstacle to teaching Timothy.

"But My Husband Is Greek"

Eunice and Lois's circumstances weren't ideal, but that didn't stop them from teaching Timothy. What if Eunice had said, "If Timothy's father were a believer, then we could memorize Scripture," or "Someday when my husband becomes a believer, then we will talk about Jesus." What if Lois had said, "I'm too old to teach; it is Eunice's responsibility. I taught her. Now she can teach Timothy." Eunice and Lois did not have a strong faith community to support their efforts, but in those less-than-ideal circumstances, they also had some positives.

They recognized an atmosphere ripe for effective teaching in the home. Plus they had a faith to share. Eunice and Lois were very capable women, probably better educated than many women in Lystra. They were able to read, to interpret, and to teach. They knew the Scriptures and were able to make a judgment about Paul's message when he came to Lystra, and they learned from him. And most importantly, they knew Jesus. They had something—and Someone—to share, and we do, too.

We are all learners, gleaning formally or informally from mentors, teachers, parents, and friends, as well as life experiences, which means we, in turn, have something to teach. The question is, are we passing on what we have learned and what we know to be true? Are we investing in others? There are people in our lives who would benefit from our knowledge if we open our eyes to see them. Eunice and Lois give us good examples to follow.

chapter twelve

Priscilla:
A Christ Follower Works with Others

Acts 18:1–28
Romans 16:3–5
1 Corinthians 16:19
2 Timothy 4:19

Have you ever noticed how little it takes to connect with someone when you are in a strange place? For example, when you are trying to merge into a new group, you feel awkward, as if you are from another planet. You attempt to make small talk, and you smile a lot. Then you meet someone who has visited your hometown or who knows your brother. The awkwardness fades.

Or suppose you move to a new place where you don't know a soul. On Sunday, even though butterflies of homesickness are swirling in your stomach, you take your daughter to church. As you are picking her up from the nursery, someone says, "Excuse me. Did you by any chance go to college in Texas?" It turns out you two were on the same campus at the same time. You begin to talk like old friends, even though in college you barely knew each other, and the butterflies disappear.

Perhaps the apostle Paul was feeling a similar need to connect when he arrived in Corinth for the first time in A.D. 50. He was spiritually and emotionally bruised from the battering he had taken so far on his second missionary journey. He expected Timothy and Silas, two of his coworkers whom he left behind in Berea, to join him eventually, but for now he was alone. He needed comfort and understanding, and he needed a job. He found all that and more when he met Priscilla and Aquila.

Match Made in Heaven

Occasionally Paul received offerings for support, but most of the time he supported himself by working. In Corinth, alone and without any financial support, he needed a job. He was a tentmaker, so he went to the area of town where tentmakers were located. Among their stalls, Paul spotted tents that he considered well made. As he ran his hands over the material and studied the seams, a woman sewing a tent watched him. When Paul looked up, she said, "May I help you?"

A conversation began. They talked "tents" and "tent-making," because Paul was interested in finding a job, and Priscilla, the woman, was interested in making a sale. Paul mentioned he was looking for work about the time Priscilla's husband joined the conversation.

Aquila said to Paul, "Do you know how to make tents?"

"Yes, I do," Paul answered.

Aquila asked, "Where did you learn to make tents?"

Paul said, "I'm from Tarsus." That's all Paul needed to say. Everyone knew Tarsus was famous for its tentmaking.

"What brought you to Corinth?"

Paul answered. "I travel a lot. I came here from Athens."

"We're not from here either. We're from Rome, and we've been here about a year."

Paul asked, "What brought you to Corinth?"

Priscilla and Aquila looked at each other. With their eyes, one said, "Should we tell him?" And the other said, "Yes."

Aquila said, "We were kicked out of Rome."

"Kicked out?"

"Yes, we're Jews. We were forced to leave."

"Why?"

As Priscilla and Aquila answered this question, Paul learned they had a third thing in common. Besides being tentmakers and Jews, they were also Christians. Priscilla explained how the Jews in Rome were in disagreement because some believed in Christ and others didn't, so the emperor, Claudius, decided to get rid of all of them.

(Let me break into the story for a minute to explain. The Bible doesn't say when Priscilla and Aquila became Christians. Many people believe that Paul led Priscilla and Aquila to Christ, but 1 Corinthians 16:15 tells us that Paul's first converts in Achaia, the territory that included Corinth, were Stephanas and his household. That added to the fact that Claudius kicked the Jews out of Rome because of a squabble over Jesus gives me the impression that Priscilla and Aquila were Christians before they met Paul. Okay, back to the story.)

Paul said, "I know what having to get out of town is like. It happens to me almost every place I go. Why, just recently in Thessalonica, a ruckus was stirred up because of my speaking, so I had to leave. From there I went to Berea and was having a good response when the Thessalonian troublemakers arrived and persuaded the people not to listen to me."

As he talked about his troubles, Priscilla and Aquila listened with understanding—the kind of understanding that brings hope to a weary soul. As Paul's tension melted, he was certain he had found soulmates. Priscilla and Aquila were likewise encouraged. After a lonely year in Corinth with no kindred spirits, here was someone who shared their Jewish heritage, their work skills, and their passion for Christ. They saw the connection as God's doing—a match made in heaven—so they said, "Come stay with us and work with us."

In accepting their invitation, Paul found what he was looking for—comfort, understanding, and a job! Priscilla and Aquila hadn't been looking, but they found new roles and new adventures as their lives intertwined with Paul's. Their lives would never be the same.

Open Heart, Open Home

Asking Paul to live with them added stress to Priscilla and Aquila's life; it always does when you add another person to your household.

More food to buy and to prepare.

More dishes to wash.

More laundry to do.

Adjustment to losing some of your personal space.

More concerns to deal with, complicating life.

Paul, as an experienced traveler, stayed in enough homes that he was probably very efficient about looking after himself, so in that sense he made a good guest. But Paul also attracted guests. Paul's mission was to win men and women to Christ, so he engaged people in dialogue wherever he was, on the job, in the marketplace, or after synagogue services. Many of those conversations couldn't be finished at the time, so it was natural for Paul to say, "I'm staying with Aquila and Priscilla. Why don't you stop by later? We can talk more about it then."

Now Corinth was an "anything goes" type of town, a wicked city noted for its drunkenness and debauchery. So some of those people who "dropped in" were not—how shall we say it—the most desirable of houseguests. Some of the people who came by—and later became believers— were fornicators, idolaters, adulterers, thieves, drunkards, revilers, and extortioners (1 Corinthians 6:9–11).

Priscilla invited them in and made them feel at home. Around her table she accommodated Paul's discussion groups and cleaned up after the guests were gone. Why did she welcome Paul and others when it added stress to her life?

Priscilla became a hostess because she was a Christ fol-lower, and she knew that having unhurried dialogue in the warm, receptive environment of a home made it possible for people to hear the gospel message. Plus, she thrived in an environment where dialogue was continually taking place and where at any time a new convert might be born. She was ecstatic when this happened.

Besides, Priscilla, whose Christian education had been cut short in Rome, learned from Paul as he talked with others in her home and in the synagogue where he held discussions (Acts 18:4). In the synagogue, the men and women were seated separately, and the women weren't allowed to say anything, but Priscilla listened closely. She absorbed what Paul said, but still she had questions, and her home was a place where she could ask them.

As they broke bread together, Priscilla asked Paul questions. "Where have your travels taken you, Paul? When did you first meet Christ? What was it like to come face to face with the resurrected Jesus? What have you learned since in following Christ? What do the Hebrew Scriptures teach about Christ? What have your troubles and trials taught you about the nature of the Christian life? Why is it important for believers to meet together? How does the Holy Spirit work in our lives? What is the meaning of the cross?"

Because she became a hostess in addition to being a tentmaker and a wife, Priscilla had her own mini university, her own school of faith right in her own home, in which she could learn and grow from her association with Paul.

As their lives became more intertwined with Paul's, he recognized the spiritual growth in Priscilla and Aquila and how much they helped him, so when he left Corinth after eighteen months, Paul took them with him. Paul planned to be in Jerusalem for Passover and then go to Antioch of

Syria to report to the church that had commissioned him to be a missionary. It was a long journey, and anything could happen along the way, but on board ship they could continue their conversations. Sometimes it was just the three of them. Other times it included other travelers on board. Paul continued as the teacher, but graduation day was coming for Priscilla and Aquila when they would be teachers, too.

The Unexpected at Ephesus

Their ship docked in Ephesus, a city with a large Jewish population. Even though he was only going to be there for a short time, Paul took advantage of this and headed for the synagogue, where he reasoned with the Jews. He said enough to whet their appetite. They said, "Please stay with us longer. We want to hear more."

Paul responded, "God willing, I will try to come back sometime. In the meantime, I'll tell you what I will do: I'll leave two knowledgeable people here with you. They can tell you about Christ. These are my coworkers, Priscilla and Aquila."

However, Paul's authority as a teacher was different from Priscilla and Aquila's. Paul was a rabbi, so he was free to expound in the synagogue, but Priscilla and Aquila were lay people and Priscilla was a woman. They could not be teachers in the synagogue, but they could teach individually—so they opened their home to inquirers.

The two who opened their home to Paul in Corinth, also opened up their home to people in Ephesus who wanted to know more about Christ. Eventually they began meeting on a regular basis and a church resulted. Once more Priscilla graciously opened her home to accommodate curious visitors, new converts, and growing Christians.

House churches weren't necessarily warm and fuzzy—not all were homogeneous congregations. Priscilla accommodated people from many different backgrounds. She didn't put a sign on her door that said, "Only people who have totally cleaned up their act can come in." Ephesus attracted visitors from far and wide, including criminals, so Priscilla welcomed them as visitors just as she did pious believers from the synagogue.

In addition to having her home ready for church meetings on a regular basis, plus drop-ins, Priscilla also had her home ready for teaching. While Paul taught at the synagogue and sometimes at lecture halls, Priscilla's classroom was her home, but as a learner herself, she still attended the synagogue. That is what she was doing when she met the person who would turn out to be her most famous student.

Apollos

At the synagogue in Ephesus, Priscilla and Aquila heard Apollos, a brilliant speaker and Jewish scholar from Alexandria in Egypt. He was an eloquent man who knew how to use language correctly and convincingly. He also was very knowledgeable about the Hebrew Scriptures (Acts 18:24), what we think of as the Old Testament. He knew how to use and apply Biblical principles, as well as teach them to others, which he did with great zeal and fervor.

Apollos sounds so capable that it doesn't seem like he needed any instruction, but he did. He didn't have a complete understanding of the Christian message. Apollos "had been instructed in the Way of the Lord, and with great enthusiasm he proclaimed and taught correctly the facts about Jesus. However, he knew only the baptism of John" (Acts 18:25).

In other words, down in Egypt, he had not heard the entire gospel story. He knew about John the Baptist preparing the way of the Lord and the baptism of repentance that he preached. But his knowledge was incomplete in some way. Many Bible scholars presume from what is said that Apollos didn't know Jesus as Messiah and Christ, or about the coming of the Holy Spirit at Pentecost.

"When Priscilla and Aquila heard him, they invited him to their home and explained to him the way of God more adequately" (Acts 18:26 NIV). As they had once taken Paul into their house, they took Apollos home with them—to their classroom. They befriended him and taught him about Jesus' death, resurrection, and the Holy Spirit. As a result, Apollos was strengthened as a believer and as a teacher. From Ephesus he went on to Achaia (where Corinth is located). He was a great help to the Christian community because "with his strong arguments he defeated the Jews in public debates by proving from the Scriptures that Jesus is the Messiah" (Acts 18:28).

Since Priscilla's name is mentioned first in the text, some scholars assume that she initiated Apollos's instruction. If that is true, she did it very tactfully. After all, she could have encouraged Aquila to question Apollos in front of everyone. If he wasn't teaching correctly, he needed to be exposed so people wouldn't be misled. She could have encouraged Aquila to interrupt Apollos, interrogate him publicly—get the issues out in the open. That approach certainly would have done that, but a potentially great teacher might have been embarrassed, humiliated, and lost to the Kingdom of God. It might have discouraged him from speaking and it might have kept Apollos from learning "the rest of the story" about Jesus, and what a loss that would have been!

Priscilla in History

As it was, Priscilla and her husband approached him as an equal and with no qualms about correcting an Old Testament scholar and noted teacher. That it was her initiative and her leadership may well be true because she made a *lasting* impression.

One of the oldest catacombs of Rome is named after her.

A church on the Aventine in Rome is also named after her.

The early church father Tertullian wrote about her, "By the holy Prisca [the more formal version of her name], the Gospel is preached."

The great German scholar Harnack thought Aquila and Priscilla wrote the book of Hebrews. He thought that was why Hebrews begins with no greetings and why the author is nowhere named—because the main author of Hebrews was a woman and a woman was not allowed to teach.

The preservation of her name and ministry both by historians and by the Holy Spirit in Scripture, particularly by her having taught Apollos, is proof of her stature and strength as a teacher.

That she might have taken the initiative, even the leadership, though, does not mean she was pushy, strident or overly concerned about her rights as a woman. Priscilla worked with others.

A Team Player

Priscilla was a woman who saw the bigger picture. She grasped what God was doing and got on board; there were others riding the same train, and she joined them and cooperated with them rather than insisting on her rights. Her thinking wasn't, "What can God do for *me?*" Rather her concern was, "What can I do for God?" We see this cooperative spirit in how she worked with her husband, with Paul, and with the church.

Priscilla's story gives us a good example of a couple serving God together. Many of the Christ followers in this book were unmarried or were widows. Priscilla and Aquila give us an example of how well two people can work together when both are committed to Christ. In Priscilla's time, women were considered intellectual inferiors, and in religious matters, most wives were simply acquiescent to their husband's faith. Priscilla never seemed to be merely an addendum to Aquila's faith. Theirs was a true partnership. Their names were always linked together. Sometimes his name was first; others times her name was first. They had a business together, they worked together, they opened their home together, and together they learned from Paul.

Priscilla's story also shows us the value of supporting ministry leaders. Priscilla and her husband worked with Paul and greatly aided his ministry. She opened her home to Paul, facilitated his teaching, supported his ministry, followed his direction, and stood by him when he was attacked. Paul was attacked in Corinth and in Ephesus on his second visit there. She and Aquila risked their lives for Paul (see Romans 16:4), even though the Bible doesn't tell us specifically what happened. The Bible does tell us that Paul and the churches of the Gentiles were grateful (Romans 16:4).

One of the last messages that Paul wrote was a greeting to this pair of Christians who had come through so much with him (2 Timothy 4:19). Other coworkers had deserted him, but these two were faithful to the end.

Priscilla worked with the church and appreciated its value. Priscilla first started opening her home in Corinth—to Paul then to the wider church community. At Ephesus she and Aquila housed a church. Her zeal for doing this did not diminish when she and Aquila moved to Rome in A.D. 54 after Emperor Claudius—the one who forced them out of Rome—died. They went back and established a church in their home (Romans 16:3–5).

Then, once again, Priscilla and Aquila were forced to leave Rome. This time it was due to Emperor Nero, who was gleefully persecuting Christians. While Nero tortured and executed Christians for refusing to denounce their faith, God led Priscilla and Aquila back to Ephesus, where once again they opened their home for ministry.

Wherever they went, their home was a center of Christian fellowship, learning, and service.

If you are a leader, you can appreciate Priscilla's example. You know what it is to need support. I hear leaders of women's ministries and missions organizations ask, "How can I get people to help? How much it would help me if I could just have someone whom I could always count on to be the greeter, provide refreshments, or clean up afterwards?"

If you are not a leader, then you can utter those wonderful words that are music to every leader's ear: "Is there something I can help you with?"

Either way, you get the picture that following Christ involves cooperation. Priscilla's life is a positive pattern for us because she was both a leader and a follower. Either way we connect with others, teamwork is important because we are to be co-laborers. Being a Christ follower is not a solo act.

Phoebe:
A Christ Follower Is a Friend to Many

Romans 16:1–2

Think of the influence of the Book of Romans—the power of its presentation of God's work in Christ and Jesus' saving power. Romans has been called the most influential theological treatise ever written. Now imagine that the apostle Paul has asked you to carry that Epistle, its ink not yet dry, to a church 800 miles away. Now you know a little about what it felt like to be Phoebe. Her role in the church at Cenchrea is unclear—was she a servant or a ruling leader of that church?—but she was at least a carrier of the gospel of Christ, as every Christian hopes to be.

Paul's letters were written on scrolls of parchment, and then someone had to be found to deliver the letter to the recipient. There was no postal system for the Roman Empire. The government had its postal system, but ordinary citizens had to find someone to carry their letters. You looked for someone who was "going that way" or who would make a special trip. Paul's courier when he sent his longest letter (which we now call the Book of Romans) was Phoebe.

Now Rome wasn't next door to Corinth, where Paul was when he wrote Romans. Phoebe had to travel by land and by sea to get to Rome. The journey was long and dangerous. Who was this woman who traveled to deliver a letter to Christians living in the capital of the Roman Empire?

Paul's Trusty Courier

All we know about her is from two verses in Paul's letter.

It was a common custom in Paul's day to send letters of commendation with a person who was traveling, or including a commendation within a letter he might be carrying. The commendation would introduce the person and testify to his character. No one among the Christians in Rome knew Phoebe, so Paul introduced her.

> "I commend to you Phoebe our sister, who is a servant of the church in Cenchrea, that you may receive her in the Lord in a manner worthy of the saints, and assist her in whatever business she has need of you; for indeed she has been a

helper of many and of myself also." —Romans
16:1–2 NKJV

Let's look closely at this commendation and see if we can
get to know Phoebe.

From her name, we can tell she was most likely a
Gentile. Phoebe is a Gentile name that comes from
Greek mythology. It means "pure" or "radiant as the
moon."

She was from Cenchrea, the eastern port of Corinth.
Cenchrea was a thriving town with temples of Venus,
Aesculapius, and Isis. The church at Cenchrea had probably been an outgrowth of Paul's work and the starting of
a church in Corinth. They were just nine miles apart.

Through hearing the gospel, either from Paul or one
of his Corinthian converts, Phoebe had left her pagan
background to become a pure and radiant light for Jesus.

Her name is not linked to a man; she is not described
as the daughter of, or wife of, or sister of someone. If you
remember, in chapter 4 we mentioned some possibilities
of what it meant if a woman's name was listed alone. It
could mean she was a widow without brothers, fathers, or
sons. It could mean that she was a very important widow,
possibly with a father or sons, but a renowned person in
her own right. Or it could mean she was a woman of
shame.

Bible scholar Mary Ann Getty-Sullivan insists in
her book, *Women in the New Testament*, that Phoebe
was a widow because she could not have acted in the
independent manner she did if her husband had been
living or if she had been unmarried. Considering Paul's

confidence in her, it is doubtful that she was a woman of shame. He had to be careful about whom he chose to send a letter with. His letters "were a kind of substitute for his presence. They had to be entrusted to people who themselves were trustworthy," according to Getty-Sullivan. Phoebe was just such a woman, as you'll see by Paul's description of her.

Sister, Servant, Saint, and Succorer

Paul spoke highly and warmly of Phoebe. He called her "*our* sister," meaning sister to all Christians—to him, to other believers in his area, and hopefully to those he was writing to. In other words, Paul was saying, "This is a woman we here all hold dear; we have a spiritual kinship, and I'm trusting you will have this same kind of relationship with her."

Paul said Phoebe was a servant, a *diakonos* of the church of Cenchrea. *Diakonos*, as noted in chapter 4, could simply mean being a servant in the sense that many believers are. They give untiringly or unselfishly to the work of the Kingdom, usually in informal and caring ways. But *diakonos* could also be an official title, suggesting a leadership role; hence, some translations call Phoebe a deacon (as the NRSV does) or deaconess (as the Williams Translation does and the NIV adds in a footnote), doing work similar to what the first deacons did (Acts 6:1–7). Either way, Phoebe would have been a woman who ministered to or served others.

Paul asked the Roman believers to receive Phoebe in a manner worthy of the saints, implying that Phoebe was a saint. As we've already noted, being a saint means called out or chosen by God. Paul spoke of her having business that she needed to attend to, something that might require the letter recipients' assistance.

Some commentaries speculate that she was traveling for business reasons to Rome. Paul found out she was going, asked her to take his letter, and she agreed. Others say that she was there on church business. They think the travel and the recommendation are associated with her role as a church leader, a servant of the church at Cenchrea. Another possibility is that she may have been traveling as a missionary or church worker.

Paul said that Phoebe had "been a helper of many," including him (Romans 16:2 NKJV). The Greek word that has been translated "helper" is *prostatis*, the feminine form of a noun that can denote a position as leader, president, guardian, champion, protectress, benefactor, or patron. That's a wide range of choices, so I looked to see how various Bible translators interpreted the word.

"a protector of many" (AAT, Beck's translation)
"a helper of many" (NASB, NKJV)
"a good friend to many" (TEV)
"a great help to many" (NIV)
"a patron of many" (ESV)
"a succorer of many" (KJV)

Evidently Phoebe cared for the affairs of others and aided them with her resources. She could have looked after them as a caring leader, in a maternal or guardian way. She could have used her influence to help people in difficult spots. If she were a wealthy businesswoman, she could have helped Christians financially as a benefactor.

From what we've learned about Phoebe from Paul's commendation, do you feel like you are getting to know her? I didn't until I got to that word "succorer." It is an old English word that describes someone who brings relief or assistance to someone in time of want, difficulty, or distress. It speaks of comfort, assistance, and outreach, so when I read "succorer of many," I began to feel like I knew Phoebe. The word pulled the other characteristics together and helped me see a woman I could recognize. I believe it is because it brought to mind women I've known who are a lot like Phoebe.

Phoebe's Modern Counterpart

Paul used one long sentence to describe Phoebe. I'll need more words to describe her 21st century look-a-likes.

These they exude a sense of knowing in whom they believe. A few of them are rich, but most of them simply have some disposable income. They may not be widows like Phoebe, but they are free to make decisions about how and when money is spent. They use their resources to help others. They become benefactors by paying rent, buying food, paying doctor bills, or supporting pursuit of an education. Besides supporting others, they get involved, serving on the board of a nonprofit organization or going on an overseas mission trip.

But these strong women also have a mothering spirit about them—not a soft, doting kind of mothering, but a looking after, protective kind of mothering. They have an umbrella outlook on life; they extend their arms wide and gather people in under their protection and care. They serve as leaders in the church; people respect their opinions. It's not that these women want to be dominant or controlling; they see it all as their service to God. As servants, they just want to help, and they have the means to help.

This Phoebe-type woman sounds almost too good to be true, yet they are out there. And we are all better off for having women like them our lives. Most of us need some "looking after" at some time or other, including Paul. Just as he counted himself fortunate to have Phoebe in his life, we can count ourselves fortunate if we have someone like her in our lives.

With the help of an archaic English word I could see Phoebe as a real person who was a sister, a servant, a saint, a traveler, a helper of many. She was someone Paul depended on and had confidence in. With such stellar qualities, why would Paul need to recommend Phoebe? Was it just a nice custom, kind of like good manners and nothing more? And why would he need to encourage Christians to give another Christian a warm friendly reception? Wouldn't the Roman Christians be eager to help another Christian? Why did Paul have to prod them to assist her?

In Need of a Good Word

Words of recommendation were important in the ancient world. People who traveled didn't have very many public facilities such as hotels or restaurants for lodging and food. Some of the facilities they did have were not well kept, so travelers depended on the assistance of people they had sometimes never met for their needs. They carried letters of recommendation with them so people would let them stay in their homes. "Hi, I know your brother, and he said if I needed a place to stay while I was in your city to look you up. See, here is a letter from him telling you about me."

Christians, too, depended on this kind of hospitality as they traveled from city to city, so they carried letters of recommendation. Their concern, though, wasn't only lodging. The letters also verified who they were and certified they were not false teachers, which Paul had to continually warn churches about. That's why, after Priscilla and Aquila taught Apollos and he decided to go to Achaia, "the believers in Ephesus helped him by writing to the believers in Achaia, urging them to welcome him" (Acts 18:27).

Beyond having a place to stay and providing credentials for a teacher or preacher, there should have been no other need for commendations among Christians. Ideally, there should be no strangers in the family of Christ. And we have seen evidence earlier where this is the case: look at how Lydia took in Paul and his traveling companions and how Paul quickly teamed up with Aquila and Priscilla. Sometimes when you meet up with another Christian, there is an immediate connecting of the spirits. And yet Christians don't always welcome other Christians with open arms. Christians can be shy, frightened, uncomfortable, or cliquish. Sometimes they like things just the way they are, and while they talk of outreach, they don't want things to change when someone different becomes a part of their fellowship. Sometimes they hold back because the new Christian in their midst is from a different culture or seems more sophisticated or less sophisticated.

To have someone say, "Hi, I'm a Christian" doesn't always make others want to embrace them. Some want to know, "What kind of Christian are you?" And more specifically, "Are you a Christian like I am?"

I was amused when one of the members of a Christian board I'm on told me she was questioned about me after I sent out some introductory letters. The recipient knew Norma and showed her the letter. Then she asked, "Is she all right?" In other words, is she a born again, conservative Christian who doesn't do anything weird? She wanted assurance from Norma, someone she knew and trusted. Even though I was a Christian—and my letter said I was—I still needed a recommendation.

If Phoebe showed up with a scroll under her arm at a gathering of Roman Christians and said, "Hi, I'm Phoebe. I'm a Christian," she might have been met with reticence and skepticism because she was a woman, because she was from Cenchrea, because they were from the capital city of Rome, or any of a number of other reasons. As it was, Paul reminded them to accept her and to help her.

When Barriers Fall

Paul was so confident of the caliber of person Phoebe was that he believed she deserved to be welcomed "in the Lord in a manner worthy of the saints" (NKJV). He directed the letter recipients to receive her and help her in any way they could.

The problem was that Paul knew Phoebe but the Roman Christians didn't know her. When Paul sent his letter to the Philippians, he sent it by Epaphroditus. The Philippian Christians knew him because they had earlier sent him to Paul (Philippians 2:25–30). But in Rome, Phoebe was a stranger meeting strangers.

But Phoebe didn't come all that way to be dismissed. This is the way I imagine it. She said, "I have a letter for you from Paul." With the mention of Paul, the group warmed up a bit. *She says she's a Christian. She says she knows Paul. Hmm…how do we know the letter she is holding is really from Paul?*

Someone suggested, "Read it." They might not quite trust Phoebe yet, but still it was a letter, and receiving a letter was a special thing.

One of the Roman Christians stepped forward, took the scroll from Phoebe, unrolled it, and began reading it out loud. As Paul's argument developed for being saved by grace, low murmuring began rumbling through the crowd. *That sounds like Paul.* While Paul hadn't been to Rome yet, many in the group such as Priscilla and Aquila had met him in other places and knew him. They knew Paul's cadence and recognized his vocabulary. If there were any lingering doubts by the time the end of the letter neared, it faded as the reader read Paul's greetings to specific Roman Christians (16:3–15). He not only called them by name, but he identified them with a specific description.

Because sending a letter was so complicated, you wanted to get the most out of your effort, so Paul often saluted particular people in his letters. He saluted many individuals in his letter to the Romans. Ears perked up as the letter reader shared Paul's greetings. The people listened for their names. We're not going to repeat the whole list here, but in keeping with the nature of this book, we're going to look at the women Paul greeted.

The first one he mentioned was Priscilla, whom you met in the previous chapter. Priscilla and her husband Aquila had returned to Rome after meeting Paul in Corinth and helping him in Ephesus. At once of those places, they had risked their lives for Paul. As the reader read Paul's mention of this, several listeners shuddered. When Paul said he was thankful and the Gentile churches were thankful to Priscilla and Aquila, many shook their heads appreciatively and said "Amen."

Then he greeted Mary of Rome. Paul needed no extra adjectives when he mentioned Mary. Hers was a common Jewish name, but her efforts on their behalf were anything but common. She excelled in her labor for the church.

They nodded in agreement when Paul said Andronicus and Junia, who had once been in prison with him, were outstanding among the apostles.

They smiled when he mentioned how hard dainty and delicate Tryphaena and Tryphosa worked. These two women worked to the point of exhaustion for the sake of the church and Christ. Another hard worker he mentioned was Persis; they all agreed, for they loved her dearly.

Paul greeted Rufus and his mother, acknowledging Rufus' work for the church and his mother for her kindness to him. They had all experienced a little of her mothering.

Name by name, as the greetings were read aloud, a cloud of emotional warmth filled the room. They felt closer to each other and more appreciative, but more importantly, they were convinced the letter was from Paul. It was authentic, and therefore Phoebe was a legitimate courier. They were now ready to receive Phoebe and assist her.

With warm hearts they received Phoebe. They greeted her with "a holy kiss" (Romans 16:16) and offered her hospitality. They offered their assistance with her business, filling her in on Roman politics and law. They honored and welcomed Phoebe as a legitimate church leader because they knew she was no alien to be barred from their fellowship. She was a friend of Paul's and a Christ follower just like they were.

Paul's commendation of Phoebe was brief. Only a line or two describes her, so you could easily overlook her, but what she did was very important. One scholar said, "Phoebe carried under the folds of her robe the whole future of Christian theology." The book of Romans, like no other document ever written, has influenced the development of Christianity and spelled out the implications of God's saving grace through Jesus Christ. There was no carbon copy or backup file. It was up to Phoebe to get the message to Rome, and she did.

On a day-by-day basis, the way we follow Him may seem insignificant and unimportant, but in God's eyes, it may look altogether different. Who knows what great purpose you may be fulfilling when you are faithfully following Christ?

chapter fourteen

Titus's Helpers:
A Christ Follower Reaches Out to the Young

Titus 2:3–5

In our study, we have looked, for the most part, at the lives of actual, named women in the New Testament; but in this chapter, we'll be looking at a developing role for women—a role needed then and needed today. The role was initiated and encouraged because the church needed mature women to reach younger women.

Places have personalities and characteristics just as people do. Sometimes it is the way people talk; for example, you'll hear "y'all" more in the south than in the north. Sometimes it is the way people take care of their property, or don't!

Sometimes people have a laid-back attitude about life so that meetings seldom start on time. In some places, people move at a fast pace; in others at a slow pace. One area may be saturated with gambling, while residents of another area may totally resist it.

Consequently, we associate places with their personalities and characteristics. The island of Crete, for example, was associated with dishonesty, greed, immorality, drinking, and general nastiness. H. I. Hester in *The Heart of the New Testament* said, "their proclivity to falsehood was proverbial." They were noted for their tricky and unreliable character and their love of money. "Wine was produced in abundance and the people, both men and women, had the reputation of being heavy drinkers. They seem also to have been in alliance with pirates who preyed upon the ships sailing the Mediterranean," Hester says.

Outsiders weren't the only ones who felt this way. A Cretan himself, one of their own prophets, spoke the truth when he said, "Cretans are always liars, evil brutes, and lazy gluttons" (Titus 1:12 NIV).

Paul started a mission church in this "anything goes" type of place, although we don't have a biblical description of when and how. Perhaps Paul had a vision for reaching this densely-populated island in the Mediterranean Sea when he passed by it on his way to Rome and imprisonment (Acts 27:7). As they sailed near the Cretan shores, perhaps the conversation among the passengers and workers was about the deceptive and unreliable character of the Cretans. The talk must have stirred Paul's heart, for after he got out of prison, he visited there, started a church, and directed Titus to supervise the work.

A Son in the Faith

Titus was a child of Gentile parents who placed his faith in Jesus after hearing Paul's teaching. Like Timothy, Eunice's son, he became one of Paul's protégés, a "true son" in the faith (Titus 1:4). Titus sometimes traveled with Paul and often assisted him in his work with churches (2 Corinthians 7:6–7, 13–16; 8:16–17, 23–24).

Paul left Titus at Crete so he could put in order that the things that still needed doing (Titus 1:5). He had his work cut out for him. Pastoring a church in Crete was not like pastoring a church in the suburbs of Jerusalem, where an ethical environment and an emphasis on holy living already existed before Christ came. The climate on Crete was anti-Christlike.

One of the challenges Titus had was helping new converts raise their standard of living. When we become new creatures in Christ, we have a new direction and a new power, but it can still be difficult sometimes to shed old habits, especially when you are living in a loose environment as the Cretans were. Converts coming out of this background had to continue to live there as they forged a new life in Christ. The environment pulled and tugged at their newfound dedication.

Compounding this problem was the influence of false teachers. Some of the false teachers were converted Jews. Crete had a considerable colony of Jewish traders, in addition to Roman officials and native Cretans. The false teachers who were Jewish stressed the law, myths, and genealogies. They wasted time on worthless controversies, and their standards for life had scarcely risen above that of their heathen neighbors. They rebelled and deceived "others with their nonsense" (Titus 1:10). They upset "whole families by teaching what they should not, and all for the shameful purpose of making money" (Titus 1:11). "They claim that they know God, but their *actions deny it*. They are hateful and disobedient, *not fit to do anything good*." (Titus 1:16, emphasis mine).

After a time of struggling with these challenges, Titus grew weary. Uncertain about how to proceed, he said, "Paul, I need your help. What do I need to do to strengthen this church and establish it as a witness on the isle of Crete?"

Paul's Advice

Paul responded, as he often did, with a letter. In this letter, he makes it clear that the whole church needed to be involved:

• Titus, the pastor,
• Older men,
• Older women,
• Younger women,
• Younger men, and
• Slaves.

They must all be teachers of "sound doctrine," which has to do with lifestyle, not simply beliefs as we might expect by the word *doctrine*. It "calls for attitudes and conduct that are a credit to 'the word of God' (2:5), such as will 'adorn the teaching of God our Savior' (2:10)," according to Evelyn and Frank Stagg, in their book *Women in the World of Jesus*.

The effectiveness of the teachers was directly related to their self-control and character. Paul linked authentic Christian behavior with sound doctrine, and he saw the two as inseparable partners in preventing moral and social chaos.

What part would women have in teaching "sound doctrine"? Here's what Paul recommended to Titus:

> "Teach the older women to be reverent in the way they live, not to be slanderers or addicted to much wine, but to teach what is good. Then they can train the younger women to love their husbands and children, to be self-controlled and pure, to be busy at home, to be kind, and to be subject to their husbands, so that no one will malign the word of God."
> —Titus 2:3–5 NIV

At what age would a woman have been considered "older"? This is an important question since "older" is a label most of us avoid. I once assigned Titus 2:3–5 to a discussion group of women ages 45–55 to see how they were relating to younger women. At the group meeting, several remarked they had not thought of themselves as the "older women." Isn't that the way it is? "Older" always means someone older than we are!

Actually, there's always someone younger than we are, too, so in that sense we are all "older women." Whatever age we are, there's someone younger than we are who could benefit from our experience and wisdom. The chronological age of a person is not as important as her character. Simply being "older" was not qualification enough for teaching.

Character Counts

If "older women" were to be teachers of "sound doctrine," three things were required.

They were to be reverent in the way they lived. They were to handle life with the demeanor of a person engaged in sacred things, like a priestess serving in a temple. There were no priestesses in Judaism or Christianity, but Paul used priestly terms to describe the conduct expected of "older women." The *Today's English Version* translates his words as behavior of "women who live a holy life" (2:3). The Williams translation says they should be "reverent in their deportment" (2:3).

They were not to be slanderers. Coming out of an environment with a proclivity to falsehood, the older women would be tempted to talk about others, spread rumors, betray confidences, or speak harshly or thoughtlessly. Rather, they should realize the power of words, that they can hurt and hinder or enlighten and uplift. When an older woman speaks, it should be that "she opens her mouth in wisdom, and on her tongue is the law of kindness" (Proverbs 31:26 NKJV).

The older women were not to be in bondage to

wine. Sound living involves self-restraint and self-control. Evidently Paul considered self-control to be an important antidote to the excesses of Cretan society. He said the older men were to be self-controlled (Titus 2:2). He said, "urge the young men to be self-controlled" (Titus 2:6). The older women were to teach the young women to be self-controlled (Titus 2:5). To do that, the older women would need to exercise self-control themselves by saying "no" to wine and malicious talk and saying "yes" to a reverent life.

Rather than to be slanderers or addicted to wine, the older women were to "teach what is good." "What is good" revolved around the home and family.

Home Economics 101

The older women were to train younger women to love their husbands and their children, to exercise self-control and be pure, to be busy at home, to be kind, and to submit to their husbands. These things are basic to strong homes—the kind of homes that would stand in stark contrast to the chaotic atmosphere of Crete. They are things every woman ought to know, but we forget and have to be reminded.

Take the need to love husbands and children. We might think, "Isn't that just something that occurs naturally?" There are those moments in marriage and in parenting in which love freely flows. When you walk down the aisle and say, "I do," you know your marriage will last forever. When you have intimate conversations with your spouse, you sense that you are soulmates.

When you hold your newborn in your arms and gaze into her eyes and snuggle her close, maternal love radiates from you. When that three-year-old says, "Mommy, come quick. I want to show you something," and you go outside and see a rose in bloom, you are filled with affection for your son.

But in between those moments may come times when your spouse or your children aren't so lovely. When your partner is stressed, he may show it by being irritated with you. He takes a simple question and turns it into an accusation. Or perhaps he changes over the course of the marriage, and you wonder, "Where was the attentive person I married?" Just as your children are cute and cuddly, they can also be demanding and petulant. Sometimes caring for them takes its toll, and you wish for a stretch of solitude so you can focus on what you would *like* to do instead of what you *have* to do.

Some of those "in-between times" can be short or can go on for months. It is for those times that a woman needs to be taught that love is an act of the will. Older women can teach younger women how to have willful love.

Wrapped up in willful love is the need for self-control and purity. Willful love means saying no to temptations and distractions. Willful love means having pure intentions and not being manipulative or deceptive. In a society where immorality prevailed, a young woman needed to say "no" to temptations and "yes" to being faithful to her marriage partner. She needed to resist concerns and interests that would rob her of her devotion to her children. (This helps us see why the teachers needed to not be addicted to wine. Could they teach self-control and not have control over their desires?)

To be at home doesn't necessarily mean a woman is happy at home. To be a homemaker makes you the CEO of your house—which is nice, because it means you are in control. *But* it also means you can waste time without a boss over you providing direction and incentive. In today's parlance, we would say that younger women needed training in time management, goal setting, and organizing.

Being kind is a grace that soothes family conflicts and helps members live in harmony with each other. It softens the domestic environment. Sometimes when my children would squabble, I would say, "What is the kind thing to do?" That's a good question to answer in all our family relationships.

Being submissive maintained order and stability within the family, plus served as a witness to pagans. In the early days of Christianity, female believers had an unusual amount of freedom, in contrast to what other women experienced. It was necessary, then, that Christian women be careful not to become insubordinate or neglectful at home. Otherwise, their actions would draw negative attention "to the Christian community, and, ultimately, the gospel would not be heard," Bonnie Thurston says in *Women in the New Testament*. To the Romans, well-run households meant a well-run state.

Paul saw these things as crucial in maintaining a Christian lifestyle among the Cretans. Paul didn't want women to "malign the word of God" (Titus 2:5 NIV). If the homes of Christians were in chaos, if love wasn't present, if truth didn't prevail, then what kind of witness would the Cretan church have?

This is not to say that women were the only ones responsible for a consistent witness. Paul encouraged Titus to set a good example "so that those who oppose you may be ashamed because they have nothing bad to say about us" (Titus 2:8 NIV). To the slaves, Paul insisted they be subject to their masters "so that in every way they will make the teaching about God our Savior attractive" (Titus 2:10 NIV). The fact is, *all* Christ followers have a responsibility to see that the Word of God is not discredited by their manner of life. That's why Paul's cautionary words to older women still need to be heeded.

Clasping Hands

As we have seen in this book, Christ followers have been called to do various ministries. But even as we are, we still should be conscious of those who are following. We can extend a hand to them, and if we want that hand to be clasped in return, we need to keep four things in mind.

Our attitude. Do we have a sense of the holy? That this is sacred work we are involved in? As we age, handling the responsibilities of each stage and responding to life's disappointments, our sense of wonder diminishes unless we are careful. We need to nurture our sense of wonder to help us see God at work in the world and to appreciate His using us in purposeful ways. We don't want cynicism and bitterness to take the place of reverence and awe.

Our words. Wisdom comes with age, and sometimes we can express it too quickly or in a manner hard to receive. It is even tempting to sit back and criticize rather than encourage. I remember one church where I was a member: the older women clustered under the balcony and watched the comings and goings of others as they entered and exited the sanctuary. They talked and gossiped. I often wondered how much better it would have been if they had prayed during that time instead. Or better yet, if they had spaced themselves out in the auditorium, giving words of encouragement to young mothers and assisting them with their children.

Our obedience. It is commonly assumed that if people can weather the temptations of youth, their characters become set and they are morally secure in their later years. But every stage of life has its peculiar temptations, and we can be tempted at a later stage about something that we might have shrugged off at one time. Sometimes we get tired of living a disciplined life and want to let go and do life our way. But if we are a Christ follower, the need for self-control is always there so that the Word of God will not be maligned or discredited.

What we share. Whatever age we are, we have something we can give to others to help them have a lifestyle reflective of Christ. We've learned along the way, and we can then, in turn, teach and train younger women. As we learned through Eunice and Lois' example, this doesn't mean we all have to do it in the same way. We can share through friendship, by example, in formal instruction, in casual conversations, by one-on-one Bible study, through mentoring, and with encouraging words. No matter what Christ followers do, they can always have daughters in the faith if they will reach out to them. It took me a while to believe this because I wasn't convinced younger women would be interested in what I had to share.

Daughters in the Faith

I attended a woman's conference where a former Miss America contestant spoke. She was in her late twenties, articulate, and of course, attractive. I'll admit that as she stepped onto the platform, I thought, *I doubt if a young attractive woman like her has anything to say that would relate to my life.* My ears perked up, though, when she said that women her age needed older women in their lives to teach them.

I didn't believe it. Looking at her and the other young women sitting around me, I didn't think any of them needed the help of a frumpy middle-aged housewife like me. They all seemed so self-confident, as if they had their lives totally under control. They didn't seem to need anyone, let alone someone older.

My interest piqued by Miss America's talk, I started asking women in their twenties and thirties if they needed older women in their lives. What I discovered is that in these modern times women still need help around the same issues Paul was concerned with when he wrote Titus.

"From an older woman, I need help with being a good wife and mother."

"I need helpful ideas in homemaking and early parenting."

"I need advice about relationships—marriage."

"I need advice on how to find time to spend with my family and husband and how to take care of my house."

"I go to a mom's support group of women my age that helps me with pacifiers and potty training, but I also want a mentor who will hold my hand and guide me down life's road."

"I need mentoring for being a godly wife from someone who is nurturing and has wisdom."

The name these respondents had for the older woman they needed varied. Many referred to her as a mentor or teacher. Others referred to her as role model or friend. Some called her "mother," and others cherished the wisdom of their grandmothers. One even sang the praises of her mother-in-law!

The older woman for some was only slightly older. For others, it was years and even decades. What made her the "older woman" was experience. She had a proven track record for handling life. The older woman had—and has—a wellspring of wisdom (Proverbs 18:4) to share with younger woman, and to share it effectively, it needs to be backed by a respectable life. When we truly follow Christ, our *actions will verify it.*

chapter fifteen

Timothy's Widows:
A Christ Follower
Considers the Old

1 Timothy 5:1–16

Have you ever agreed to do something and then found yourself overwhelmed? Maybe you took on a job that needed to be done but which wasn't supposed to be difficult. You were told, "There's nothing to it," but you soon found out, "There's a lot to it!" Or maybe you assumed a position because someone had confidence in you. You didn't want to let him down, even though you were aware of your inexperience. Maybe Timothy, Eunice's son, felt the same way when Paul left him in charge of the church at Ephesus. For some time Timothy had traveled with

Paul, learning much in the process, but now he was on his own, leading a church full of problems:

- Loss of focus from love and purity
- Teaching false doctrines
- Devoting themselves to myths and genealogies
- Proud, arrogant, contentious, and greedy leaders
- Administrative and organizational problems.

Paul was aware of these problems and counseled Timothy accordingly, but later, as Paul traveled to Macedonia, he realized he might not have said enough. He wanted to encourage Timothy and give him more instructions, so he wrote to Timothy.

In his letter, Paul linked the solving of some of the church's problems with various groups within the church: overseers, deacons, elders, slaves, and widows. It is this last group we are interested in because it offers us an exemplary example of what it means to be a Christ follower.

The Ephesian Widows

As you may recall from earlier chapters, widows had few ways of providing for themselves in the first century. A woman's ability to earn money—and therefore support herself—was limited. There was no governmental system of social security or welfare; and even though some general charity may have been practiced, it certainly was not organized on a wide scale.

The church realized widows needed help and accepted the responsibility. This was true from its first organizational days in Judea (Acts 6:1–6, 9:39–41).

Family was family; God's people care for each other and look after each other. The very first office-bearers whom the church appointed had the duty of caring fairly and justly for the widows (Acts 6:1–6). This attitude of caring and support attracted many widows, but the church's resources for caring for them wouldn't always stretch to cover the needs. In Ephesus, the church was close to being burdened down by the care of widows (1 Timothy 5:16). In his inexperience, Timothy wondered, *How do I solve the problem of the widows?*

Paul's Solution

Paul could have said to Timothy, "If you can't support all the widows, support none of them." But he didn't. Instead Paul reminded him that God never intended for all widows to be supported by the church. Widows with relatives should be looked after by their relatives (1 Timothy 5:4, 8, 16). This is what is "good and acceptable before God" (1 Timothy 5:4 KJV). "If anyone does not provide for his own, and especially for those of his household, he has denied the faith and is worse than an unbeliever" (1 Timothy 5:8 NKJV). The church's charity shouldn't be an excuse for children to avoid their responsibility. The support of parents and grandparents was an essential part of Christian duty.

Paul instructed Timothy to encourage the younger widows to remarry. This way they wouldn't become a burden to their families or to the church.

This left the older women without any family members to care for them. They are the ones who should be provided for by the church. As various Bible versions describe them, they are the "real widows." This doesn't mean the other widows did not feel the pain of their loss or that Paul was trying to minimize their difficulties; it was a matter of what the church could and should do. They were to help those really in need, those who were truly destitute.

With that said, Paul's writing becomes fuzzy—at least, to us. I'm sure his message was perfectly clear to Timothy, but we aren't privy to previous conversations they might have had. We don't know enough about the church at Ephesus to know for sure what Paul meant when he talked about a "list of widows" (1 Timothy 5:9, 11). Some scholars see this group—those on the list—as the widows deserving of being supported financially by the church. The implication is, if "real widows" were going to be supported, they needed to be worthy of support.

Other scholars see the "list of widows" as an organized group—female church leaders set apart for special duties and supported by the church. This group may have been the beginning of an order of widows who ministered to the church for several centuries.

Regardless of which explanation is correct, the women had to qualify to be on "the list."

What Was Required

Paul began the list of qualifications with a number—the kind of number many women don't want to acknowledge—their age! He said, "Do not add any widow to the list of widows unless she is over sixty years of age" (1 Timothy 5:9).

If you are like me, you are thinking, *What's age got to do with this?* It may have been a cultural thing. While we do not consider sixty a revered age, it was in Paul's day. Sixty and above was, according to William Barclay, "considered to be specially suited for concentration on the spiritual life. Plato, in his picture and plan for the ideal state, held that sixty was the right age for men and women to become priests and priestesses. The religious people of the East regarded sixty as the right age to retire from the ordinary activities of the world in order to engage in a life of contemplation." In addition to being over sixty, the women should have the following characteristics.

They should be capable of long-term commitment and fidelity. They should have been married only once and have been faithful to their husbands (1 Timothy 5:9). In their world, the marriage bond was lightly regarded and almost universally dishonored. In contrast, these women would have been faithful to their spouses and committed to marriage. That meant they could keep vows, something younger widows might find difficult to do. In the first flashes of sorrow and grief after the loss of a husband, a young woman might impulsively decide to remain a widow all her life and vow to dedicate her energies to serving Christ and the church. But later, as she adjusted to her loss, she might regret having taken the vow and/or forsake it all together (1 Timothy 5:11–12).

They should be known for good works. What are

you known for? Everyone has a reputation of some kind. These women were to be noted for their good works, rather than being gossips or busybodies (compare 1 Timothy 5:10 with 5:13). Their reputation would speak about how they spent their time, what their attitudes were, and whether they were worthy of respect and honor.

They should be nurturers. If the women were nurturers, then it would show in how they brought up their children (1 Timothy 5:10). In that day and time, there would have been few women of sixty who had not brought up children, either her own or someone else's. With men and women changing spouses with bewildering rapidity, children were unwanted. Consequently, according to William Barclay in *The Daily Study Bible*, "children were collected by conscienceless and unscrupulous people and, if they were girls, were brought up to stock the public brothels, and if they were boys were trained up to be slaves or gladiators for the public games." Christians rescued such children, so even if a woman hadn't had children of her own, she could qualify by having raised children such as these.

They were to be hospitable. Having an open door and open home was very important in the early church, as we have noted in earlier chapters. The homes of Christians were the first meetinghouses. Travel between Christian communities was frequent for evangelistic and teaching purposes. Inns were few and badly equipped. They were dirty, expensive, and notoriously immoral. Having a heart that would understand the importance of hospitality and practice it was very important to the work and growth of the church.

They must be willing to perform humble tasks. A courtesy associated with hospitality was seeing to it that the feet of guests were washed. People in that area wore sandals, and as a result, their feet became dusty and needed cleansing. A slave, if there was one, performed this menial task for a guest; otherwise the wife did it. So if a woman was hospitable to Christians ("saints"), then more than likely she would have washed their feet, proving she had a servant attitude.

They should be people-helpers. They should work to relieve the afflicted, assist those in distress, and help people in trouble. This could have included standing by those in trouble for their faith. When this letter was written, Christians were experiencing persecution. Paul had already been imprisoned for his faith, and by the time he would write a second letter to Timothy, he would be in prison again. Other believers were persecuted, too. To help these people was no simple matter, because if you did, you identified yourself with them and consequently were at risk of being convicted and imprisoned, too.

They must be diligent about doing good. To be numbered among the widows worthy of support, a woman must be a hard worker. She must be devoted to doing good works. She should commit her energies and time to serving Christ and the church.

As you read through the requirements, can you form a picture of these women in your mind's eye?

Real Women with Real Relevance

In the staccato way that Paul lists the requirements, you could get the impression that he was just laying down rules for the sake of listing rules, but that wasn't the case. Paul had actual women in mind—women in the Ephesian church whom he had known and worked with. We don't know their names, but in our mind's eye we can see them. Some are stooped, most are wrinkled, and some have age spots, but they glow with love that comes from selfless living.

Your ability, though, to see these women may be blocked by your reaction to the requirements. Your twenty-first century mind may be bristling. Why just the wife of one husband? Couldn't a divorced woman or a woman who had never married be on the list? Why wasn't it enough just to bring up children? Why must they be brought up *well*? Would there be anything left of a woman if she devoted all her time to good works? What about having a balanced life? Wasn't Paul asking too much?

Your vision may also be obstructed by your regard—or disregard—of older women. Some people write off older women as boring and uninteresting. Or you may like older women, but you have a strong aversion to aging. As one acquaintance said, "I love little old ladies; I just don't want to be one."

I think the disregard for old age is one reason why you seldom see this passage referenced or written about, whereas Paul's words to Titus about older women, the ones we looked at in the last chapter, are seen everywhere. Whole books are written about Titus 2:3–5.

Manuals for women's ministries make much of the passage, but I haven't seen that kind of exposure regarding this passage.

Older women want to share what they have learned, and younger women need their counsel, so both groups readily identify with Titus 2:3–5. It has appeal. But no one wants to be a widow, and hence the Timothy passage lacks the kind of connecting appeal that motivates us to appropriate it in our lives. Besides, churches don't financially support widows any longer, and if they did, they wouldn't dare make such stipulations about whom to support. It would be discriminatory! Surely there's not much to learn from Paul's words to Timothy about widows. In fact, one commentator said as much about this passage. He said it has no particular relevance for our day. I disagree.

Still Relevant

I believe Paul's words to Timothy about widows are pertinent for us to study and to apply for several reasons.

1. The description of Timothy's widows reminds us of what it means to be Christ followers. In the qualifications for those who would be supported by the church, we see qualifications for the life of every Christ follower, because Jesus had these qualities. Jesus was *committed and faithful* to the task before Him. Jesus was *known for good works*—relieving suffering, delivering sight to the blind, and setting the demon-possessed free. Jesus was *involved with children*; He took little children in His arms and blessed them. Jesus was *hospitable*. He didn't have a home to call His own, but He was concerned about guests being cared for—the guests at a wedding, the people who listened to Him for so long that they needed to be fed, and so on. Jesus was *willing to perform humble duties*. When Jesus washed the feet of His disciples, He said, "Now that I, your Lord and Teacher, have washed your feet, you also should wash one another's feet" (John 13:14 NIV). Jesus *helped people in trouble* and was *devoted to doing good*. He "took the nature of a servant....and walked the path of obedience all the way to death—his death on the cross" (Philippians 2:7–8).

2. Applying the spirit of the passage would enhance the lives of widows. Paul's overriding theme for his instructions was to "honor widows" (1 Timothy 5:3 KJV). To honor widows is to give them public regard and consideration. It is to respect and to esteem them, recognizing their wisdom and experience. Honor may also mean aiding them with financial and practical support. How encouraged and strengthened widows would feel if they were honored!

3. Applying the spirit of the passage would give all women more optimism about their future. Eighty percent of all married women will be widowed at least once in their lifetimes. What if they knew that when their husbands died, there would still be people who would honor them? What if there were a special role or responsibility reserved for widows, as the "list of widows" implied for the Ephesian widows? Think of the shift that would make in women's thinking toward the future. They would know that at a time of loss of identity they would be women of worth. Their gifts would be recognized, used, and appreciated. Their lives would have purpose.

4. Studying about the Ephesian widows reminds us that what many women do counts. Many of us do the kind of work described by Paul as qualifications to be a woman honored by the church. Those qualifications sound very much like the work women traditionally do—look after children, do humble tasks, practice hospitality, and look after people who are hurting or in trouble.   Even   if we have a powerful job with many people working for us, we still have relatives, friends or children to look after. Women are primarily the ones responsible for caregiving, but if this kind of work qualifies a woman for a special ministry—as Paul stipulated that it did—then this elevates the everyday work of our lives. It makes it God-valued work.

5. Studying this passage reminds us that in God's eyes, women "shall still bear fruit in old age; they shall be fresh and flourishing" (Psalm 92:14 NKJV). The widows had specific work to do, work that would make a valuable contribution to the church. Their work would help solve the problems of the Ephesian church.

Some scholars said the work the widows did was the work described in the requirements. They saw the women as having a ministry to children, strangers, and hurting people. They probably went to where the needs were, visiting from house to house (1 Timothy 5:13). Other scholars say theirs was a ministry of prayer (1 Timothy 5:5). Like Anna, whom you met in chapter 4, they interceded for the needs of others.

Whether it was one or the other or both, it would explain the stringency of the requirements. As the widows went from home to home, their lives should reflect the church and the Christ they served; therefore they should "be blameless" (1 Timothy 5:7 NKJV). Their lives should be distinctive from the lives of other Ephesians. The culture was in disarray; marriages weren't honored and children were unwanted. Ephesus was full of superstition and included a high criminal element. Christians were to have a lifestyle that set them apart from others, a lifestyle that would identify them as Christ followers. Consequently, Paul didn't want anyone to "find fault with them" (1 Timothy 5:7). Neither did he want to give the church's enemies a "chance of speaking evil" against them (1 Timothy 5:14). Paul didn't have high standards for just the widows. This is a theme running through his instructions to the overseers, the deacons, and elders. The church's reputation and witness could easily have been injured if those who represented the church—or who were being supported by the church—lived questionable lives.

But if the women's work was interceding, their experience in child rearing, hospitality, and helping the troubled gave them an understanding heart so they could readily identify with those asking for prayer. They could pray with compassion. Their diligence would help them persist in prayer. Their purity would give them power in prayer.

This passage, rather than weighing us down by stringency, should remind us that when we take care of the hurting and the afflicted, or when we intercede for others, we are doing Christ's work, and God meets us in the process, bringing vitality to our lives. The stringent qualifications were an avenue to life—not a life as in "I'm breathing," but a life of stimulation and purposefulness.

The widows had a choice; they didn't have to spend their remaining years serving the church. They could have given themselves over to a life of pleasure, but Paul said, "She who lives in pleasure is dead while she lives." (1 Timothy 5:6 NKJV) A woman who gives herself to pleasure dies prematurely. She's still alive physically, but the light has gone out of her life. To serve Christ is to bring a heightened sense of delight to life; it is to feel fully alive.

Bibliography

Barclay, William. *The Daily Study Bible*. Edinburgh: The Saint Andrew Press, 1960-1964.

Berry, Jo. *The Priscilla Principle: Making Your Life a Ministry*. Grand Rapids, Michigan: Zondervan, 1984.

Bruce, F. F. *The Book of the Acts, The New International Commentary on the New Testament*. Grand Rapids, Michigan: Wm. B. Eerdmans, 1966.

Burkett, Larry. "Be prepared for widowhood," *Word & Way*, June 12, 2003, page 4.

Coble, William B. *Advanced Bible Study*. Nashville, Tennessee: The Sunday School Board of the Southern Baptist Convention, January, February/March 1977.

Deen, Edith. *The Bible's Legacy for Womanhood*. Garden City, New York: Doubleday and Co., Inc., 1969.

Fitzmyer, Joseph A. *The Anchor Bible: "The Gospel According to St. Luke (I-IX)*. Garden City, New York: Doubleday and Co., Inc., 1981.

Getty-Sullivan, Mary Ann. *Women in the New Testament*. Collegeville, Minnesota: The Liturgical Press, 2001.

Gloer, W. Hulitt. *As You Go...An Honest Look at the First Followers of Jesus*. Macon, Georgia: Peake Road, 1996.

"Headlines from Headquarters," *Progress*, June/July 1999, pages 56-57.

Hester, H. I. *The Heart of the New Testament*. Liberty, Missouri: The William Jewell Press, 1950.

Liefeld, Walter, and Ruth A. Tucker. *Daughters of the Church*. Grand Rapids, Michigan: Zondervan, 1987.

Lockyer, Herbert. *All the Women of the Bible*. Grand Rapids, Michigan: Zondervan.

McBeth, Leon. *Women in Baptist Life*. Nashville, Tennessee: Broadman Press, 1979.

Meyers, Carol, general editor with Toni Craven and Ross S. Kraemer, associate editors. *Women in Scripture*. New York: Houghton Mifflin Co., 2000.

Miller, Ellen. "Sewing soothes souls," *The Times-Mail*, Bedford, Indiana, January 11, 2003, page A3.

Owens, Virginia Stem. *Daughters of Eve*. Colorado Springs, Colorado: Navpress, 1995.

Saunders, Ross. *Outrageous Women, Outrageous God*. Alexandria, Australia: E. J. Dwyer, 1996.

Shepard, J. W. *The Christ of the Gospels*. Grand Rapids, Michigan: Wm. B. Eerdmans, 1956.

Smith, Brenda Rick. "From Tragedy to Triumph," *Missions Mosaic*, April 2003, pages 10–13.

Stagg, Evelyn and Frank. *Women in the World of Jesus*. Philadelphia, Pennsylvania: The Westminster Press, 1978.

Summers, Ray. *Commentary on Luke*. Waco, Texas: Word Books, 1972.

Thurston, Bonnie. *Women in the New Testament: Questions and Commentary*. New York: The Crossroad Publishing Company, 1998.